Published by Zoographico Press

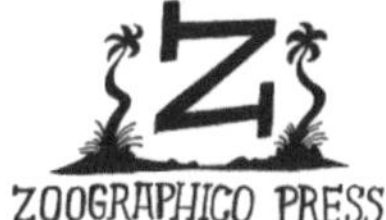

ZOOGRAPHICO PRESS

Book design by Kelly Harminc
Printed in the United States of America

www.cbmurphy.net

Two Shows at The Phipps Center for the Arts
MYSTERY LAND I PAINTINGS & MAGICAL OBJECTS

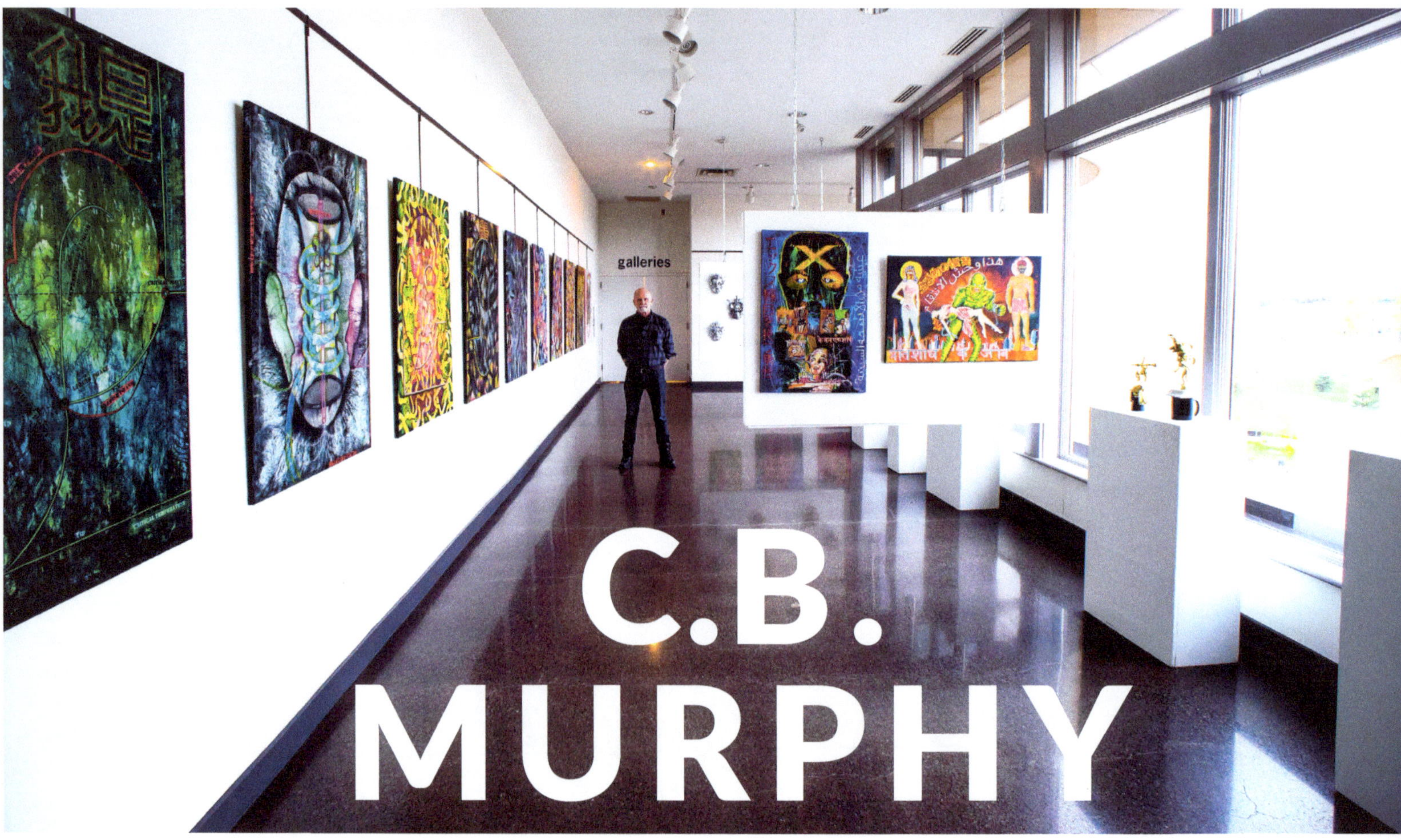

This book highlights the work of C. B. Murphy in two comprehensives shows, both held at the Phipps Center for the Arts in Hudson, Wisconsin. First opened in 1983, then doubling in size in 1992, The Phipps has made significant contributions in the in creative landscape of the greater Minneapolis and St. Paul area.

I don't see myself as creating out of nothing. I prefer the idea that I receive, respond, decode, and translate messages playfully into projects I want to work on. The seeds of the project come from the unconscious via spontaneity, and sprout in the dirt of actual processes like painting. I do my best to manifest the obscure occult impulse. Like planting seeds from a packet with no label, I don't know what will grow.

As the project evolves, I guide it by alternating between control and chaos to help it emerge from a place of mystery into a manifestation in the physical world.

The evolving form forces me to make decisions, but does not require judging. I am a merely the messenger and the message could be either beautiful, or concern death and decay — which is to say impermanence, a reminder of our brief habitation of this body.

Often the message is paradoxical and as complex as an organic form. While it can inspire it is also a reminder that every form must die. How long will it live? Who will see it? Does it matter? In the end, nothing is tragic. All is message.

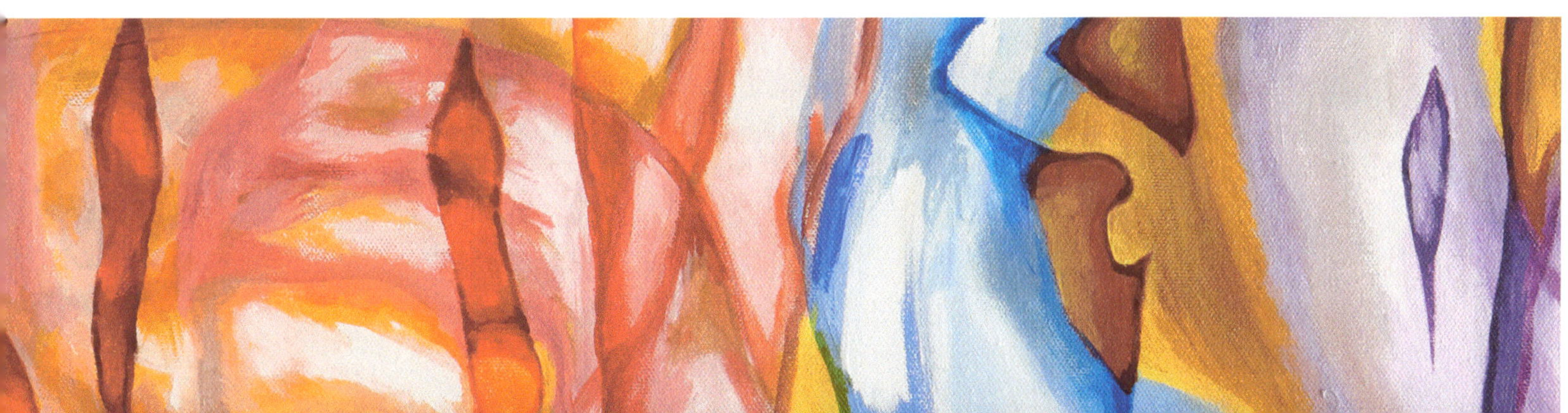

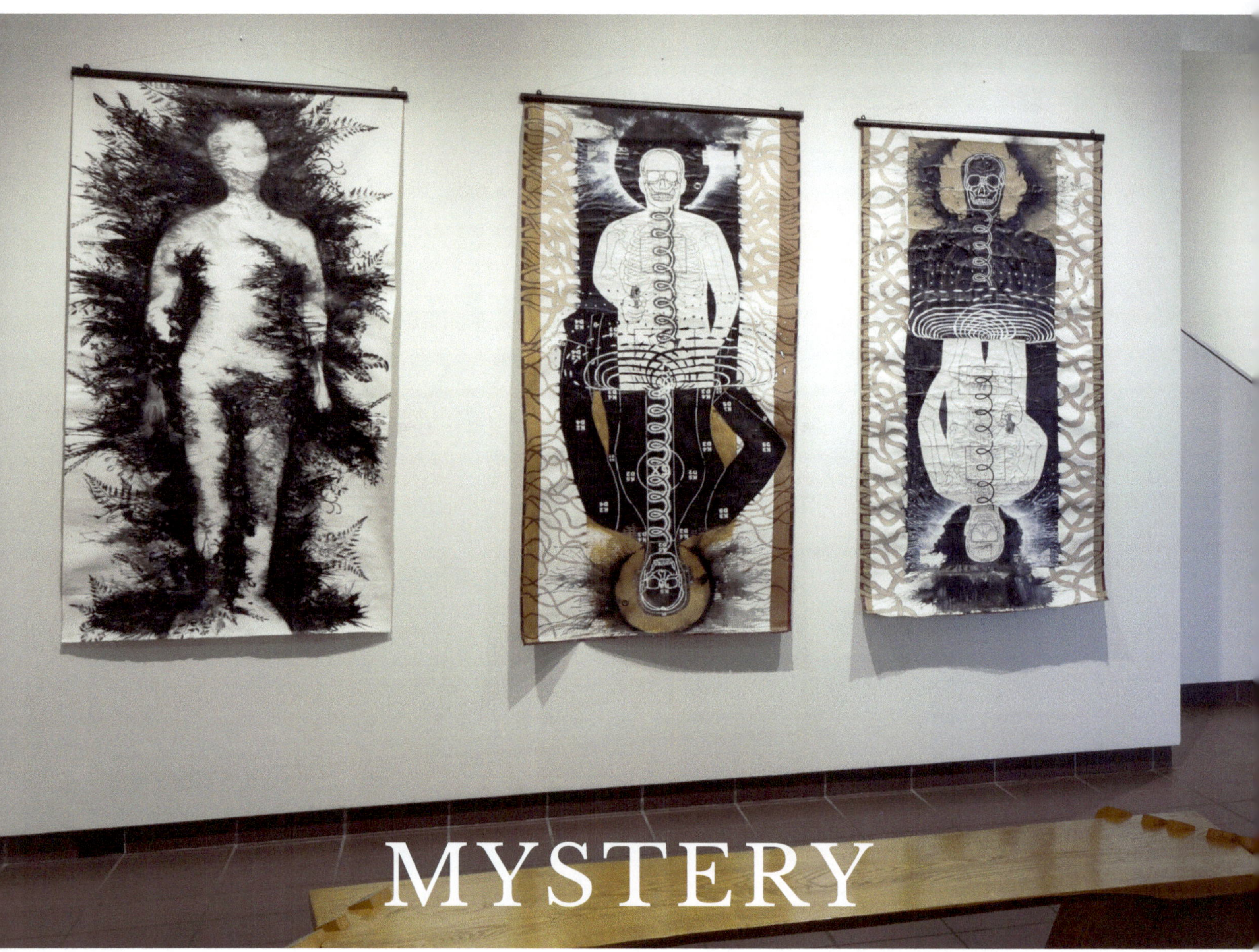

MYSTERY

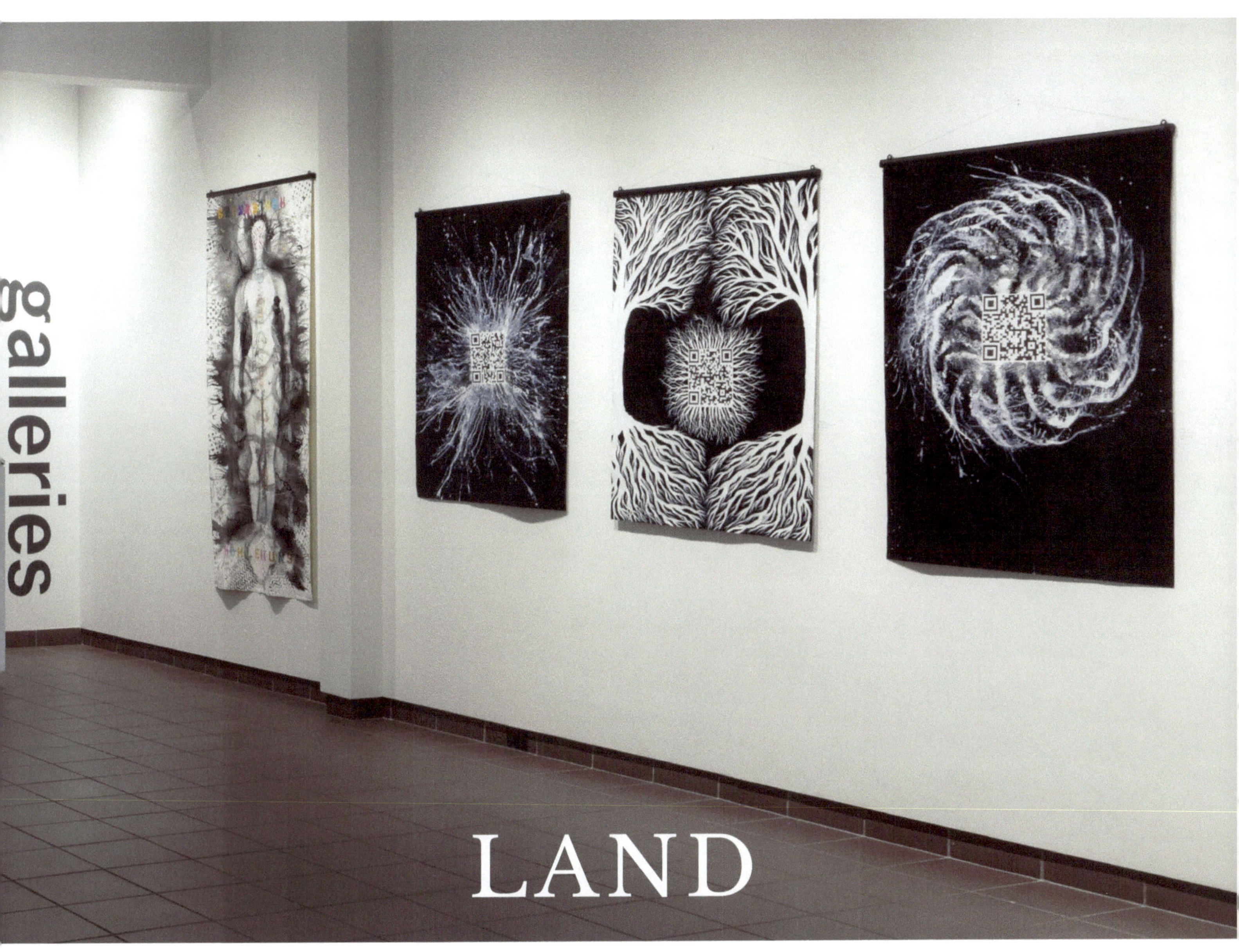

LAND

Phipps Center for the Arts, Hudson, WI 11/23/22—1/8/23

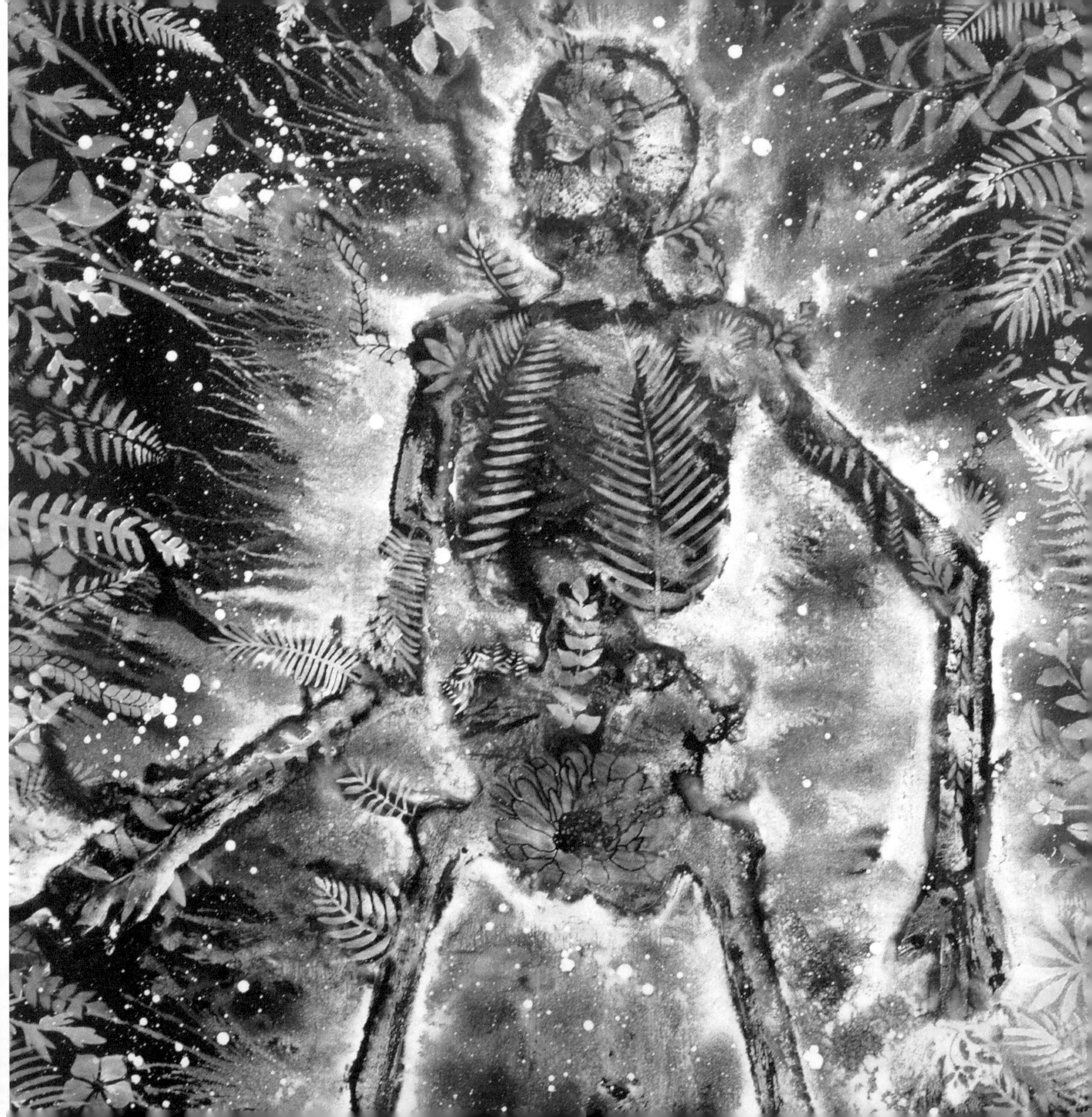

MYSTERY LAND

The Mystery Land show was exhibited (12/10/22 — 1/10/23) at the Phipps Center. It included selections from following series: QR Paintings, Saints in the Garden, Magical Charts, and Targets. The show was largely black and white, though a few paintings had muted colors, and all were designed and hung in the "banner style" of canvas or vinyl hanging from a rod.

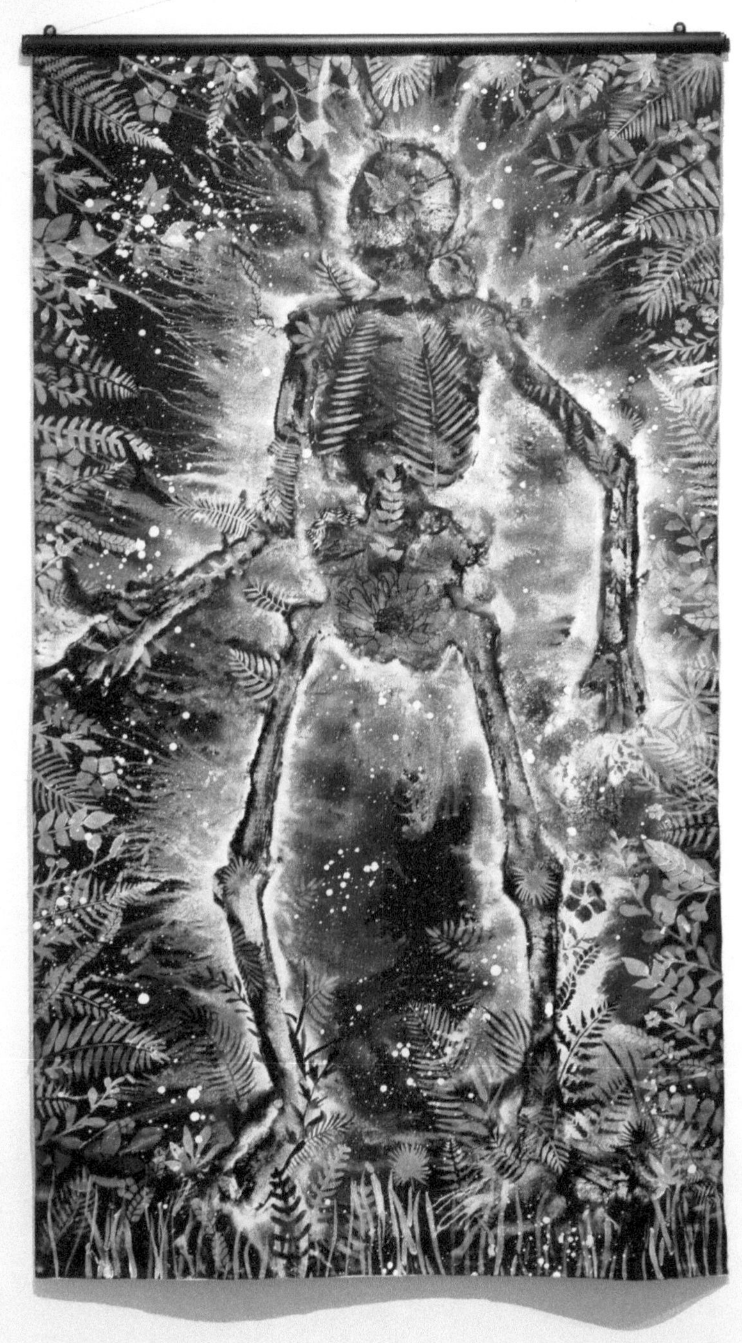

In the Year 2525

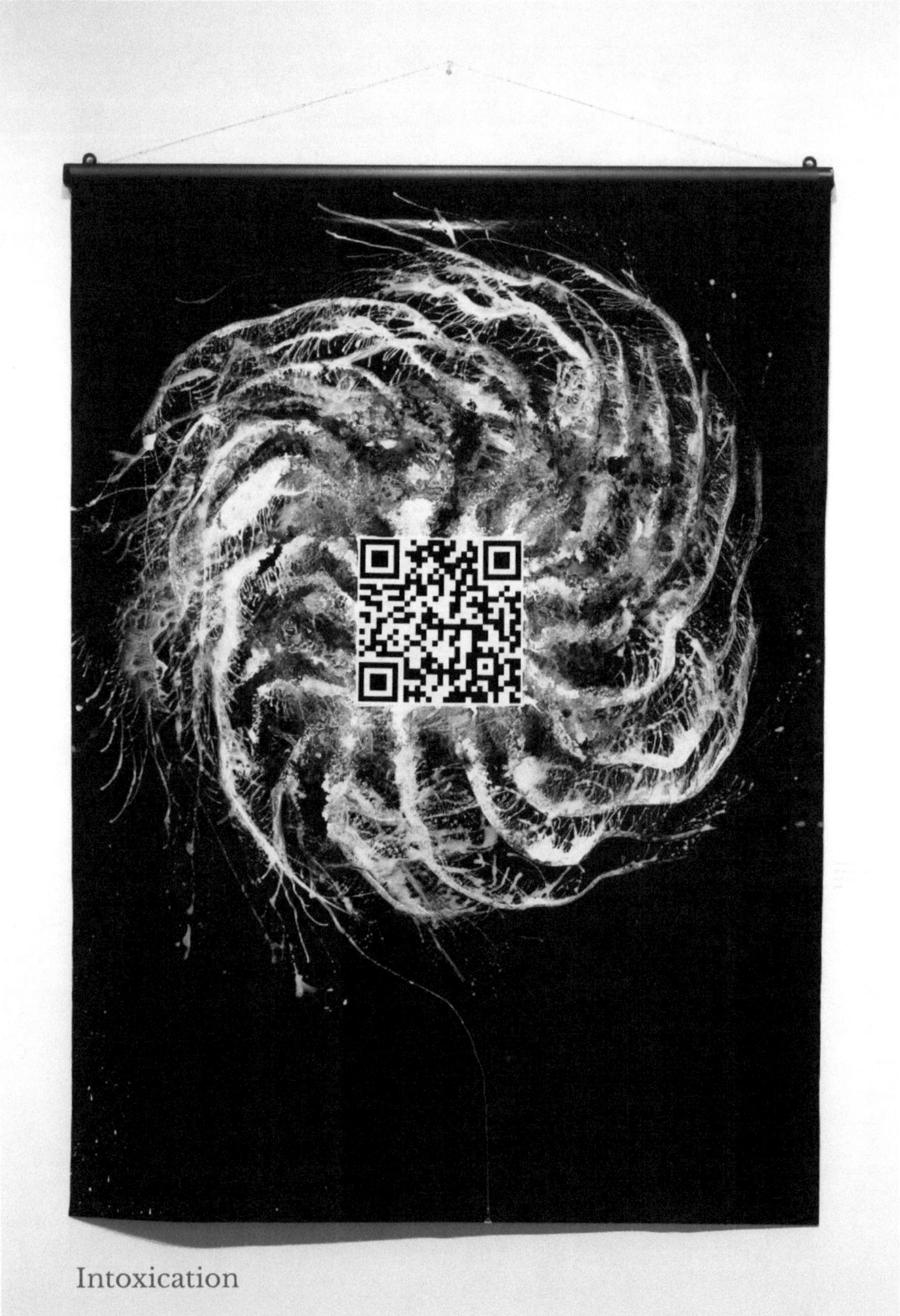

Intoxication

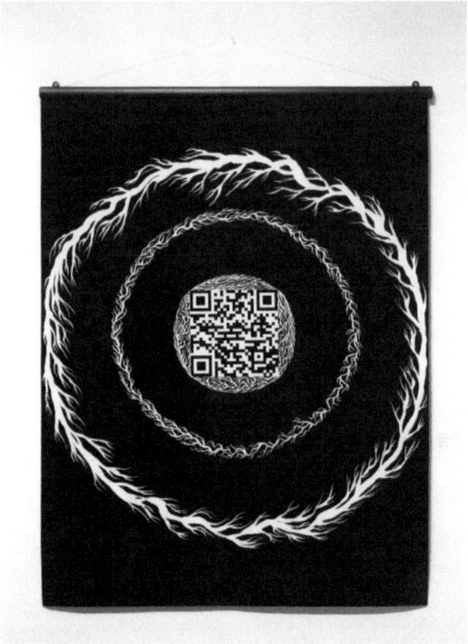

Extinction

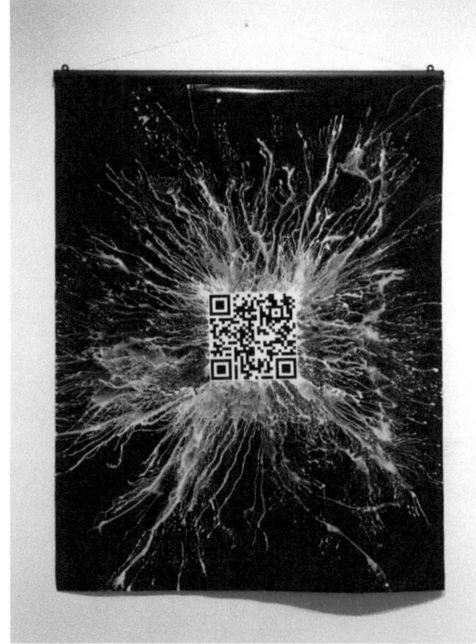

Germs

THE QR SERIES

Murphy wanted to go back to the simplest drawing forms. He began working with white acrylic on black, starting on canvas, then moving to vinyl. Always fascinated by the hypnotic interlocking of roots and branches, he began with a proscenium stage of trees on either side of an empty black center. The object that jumped out at him to fill the void was the omnipresent "QR" (quick response) code found on everything from products to menus. Graphically unique, yet evocative of a postmodern coding needing translation by our handheld devices, the QR code seemed a perfect high-tech foil to the naturalness of the plant components. At first, it was enough to see the generic QR sitting there, but he realized that the code had to be a destination. Calling on his skill and history as a filmmaker, Murphy composed short videos for each piece, concentrating on juxtaposing classic post-war fears from the great B movies of the 1950s with the more contemporary cultural concerns. In other words, an alien invasion fear merged with the fear of pandemic viruses.

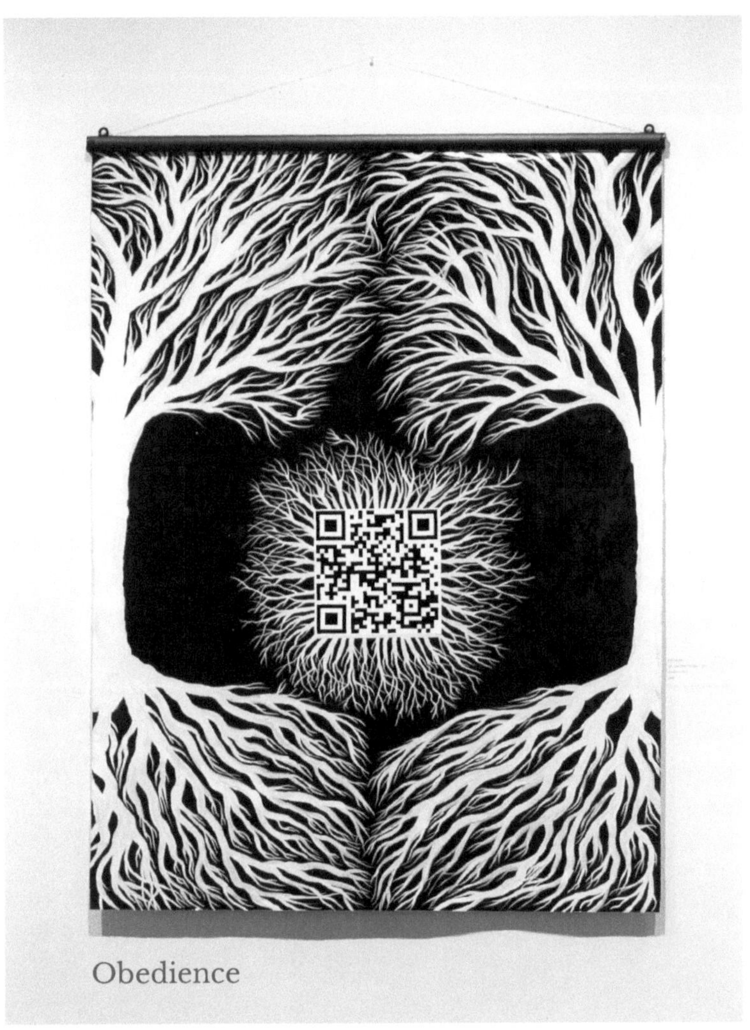

Obedience

The QR codes in the paintings link to short videos by the artist hosted on his site.

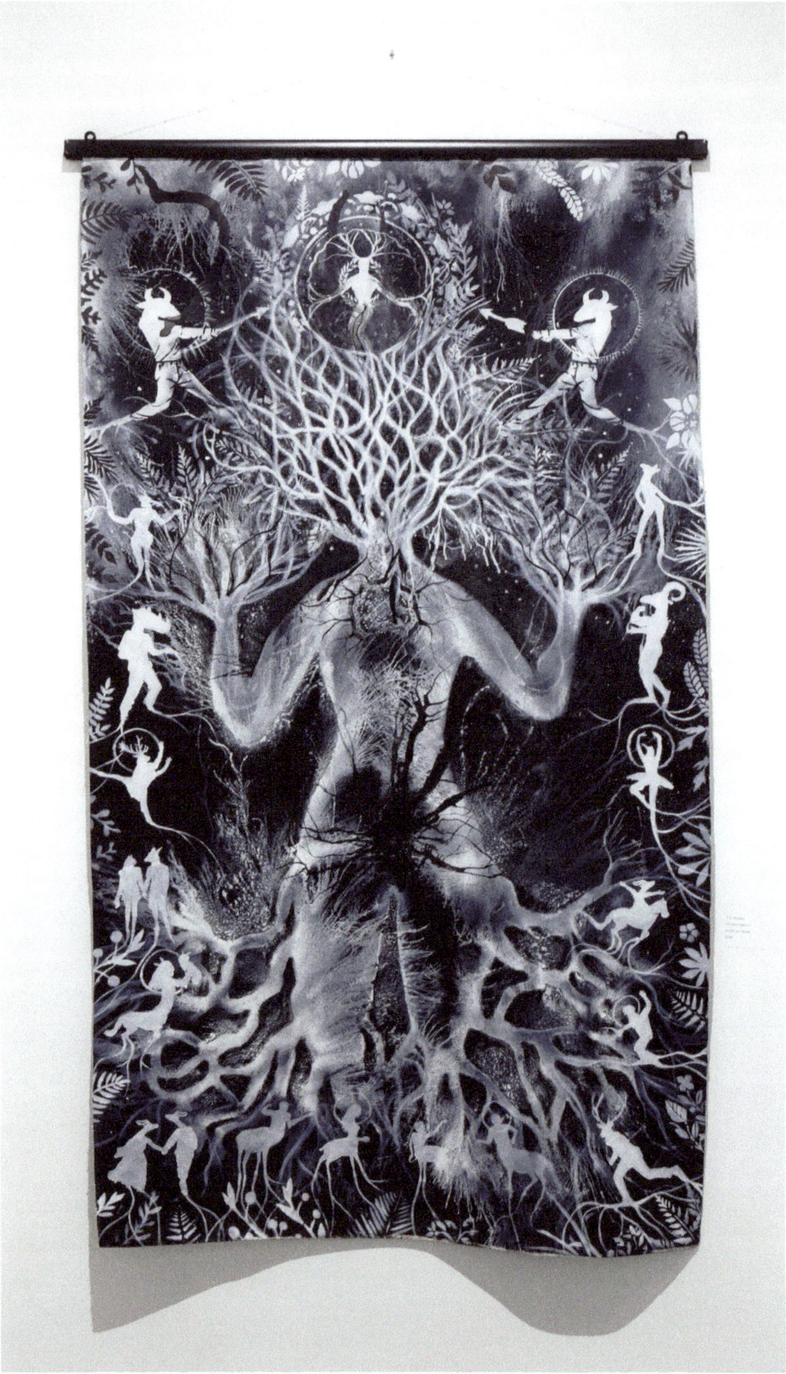

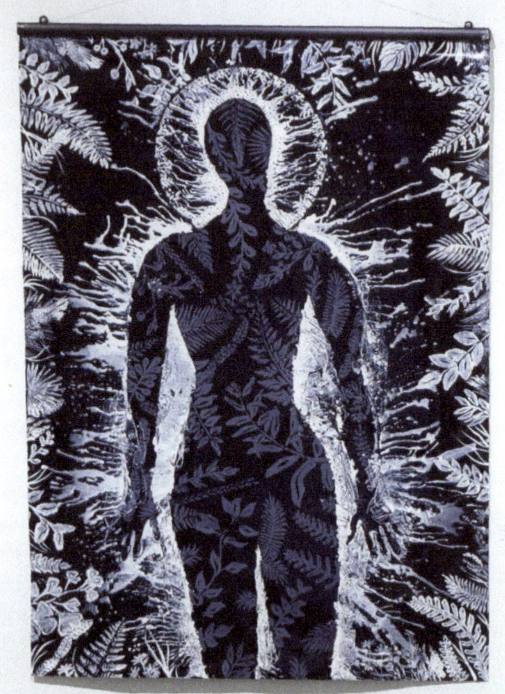

Vinyl Visitor

Saturn's Children

SAINTS IN THE GARDEN

Murphy found himself working with analogies to the visitations by otherworldly beings as seen in "spirit photography" and seances of the late 19th and early 20th centuries. These visitors appeared as ectoplasmic ghosts, humanoid, often female shapes composed of ferns, grasses, and flowers as they appeared under a full moon. Working with stencils and paints, Murphy outlined these forms by blowing and spraying paint until they appeared not unlike a photographic image developing in a chemical bath. It is unclear who these beings are. Some seem to have halos, but others can be interpreted as emanating a neutral or even predatory energy. They are some of this most accessible works of simple beauty.

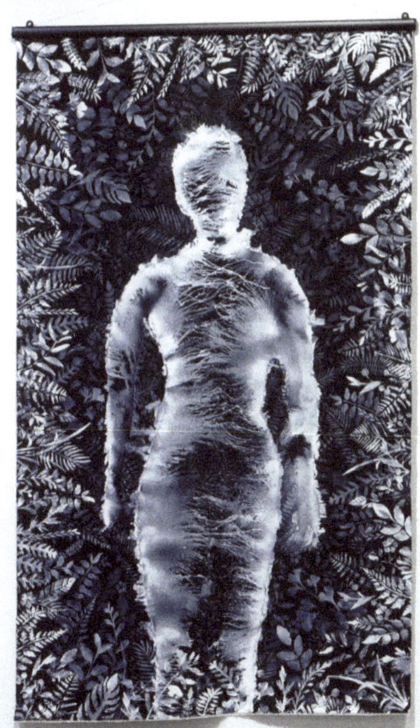

Garden Visitor

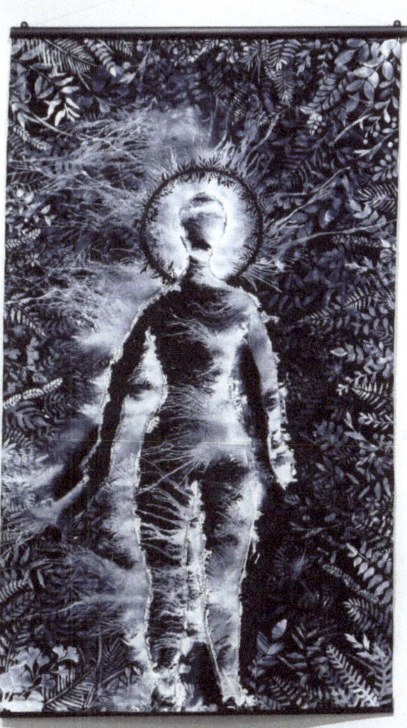

Garden Ghost: Wind

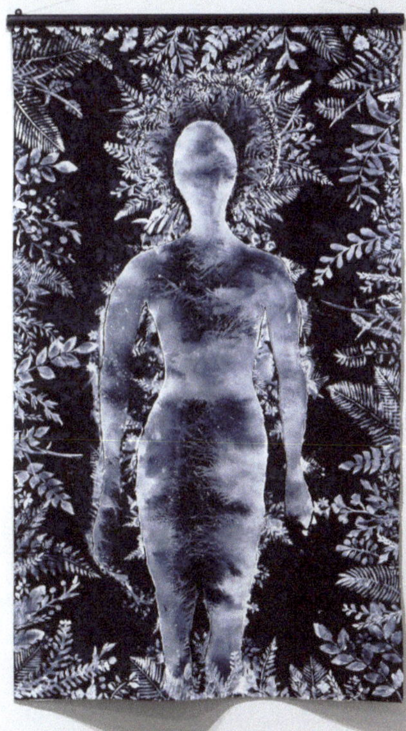

Garden Ghost: Halo

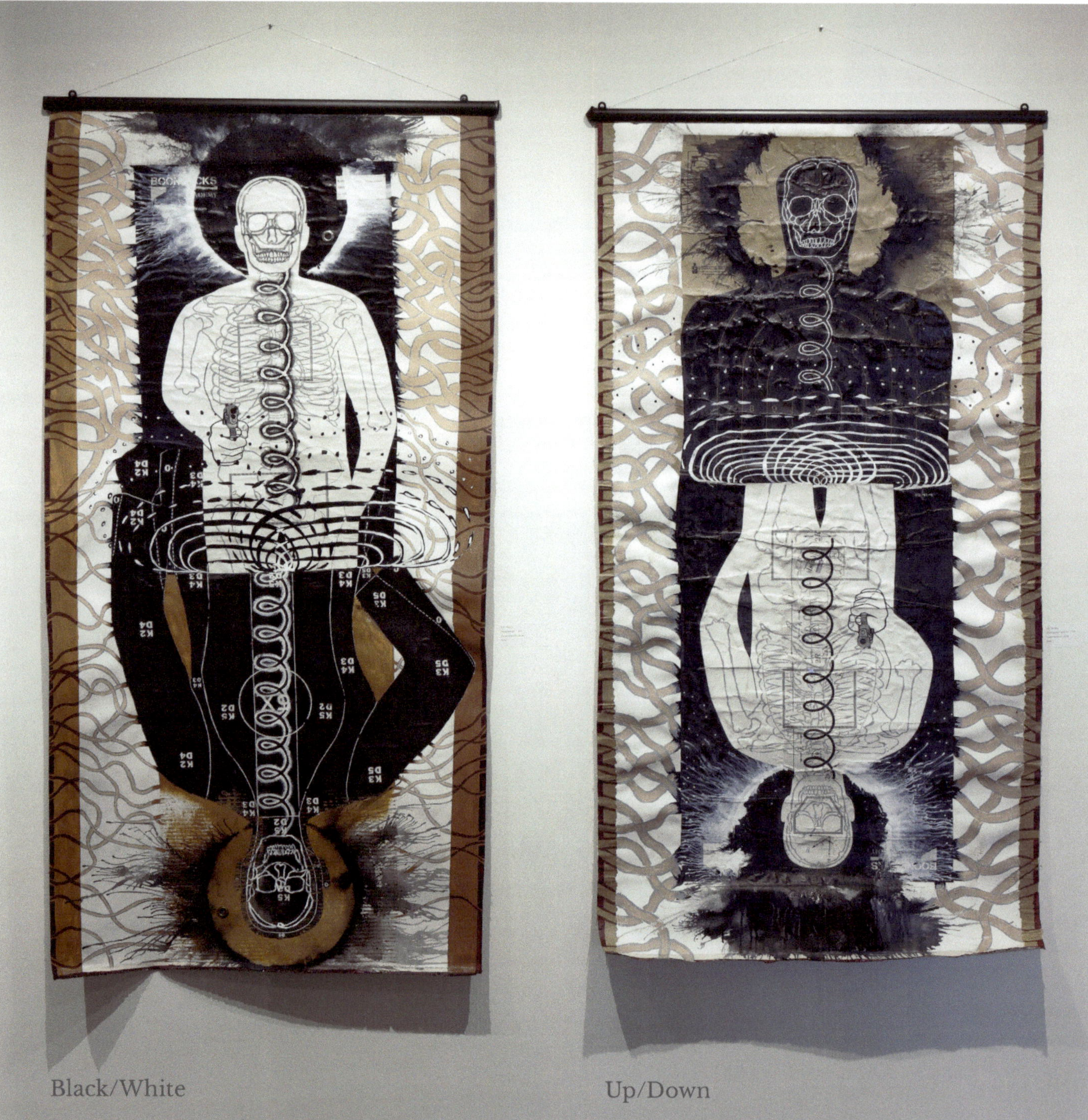

Black/White   Up/Down

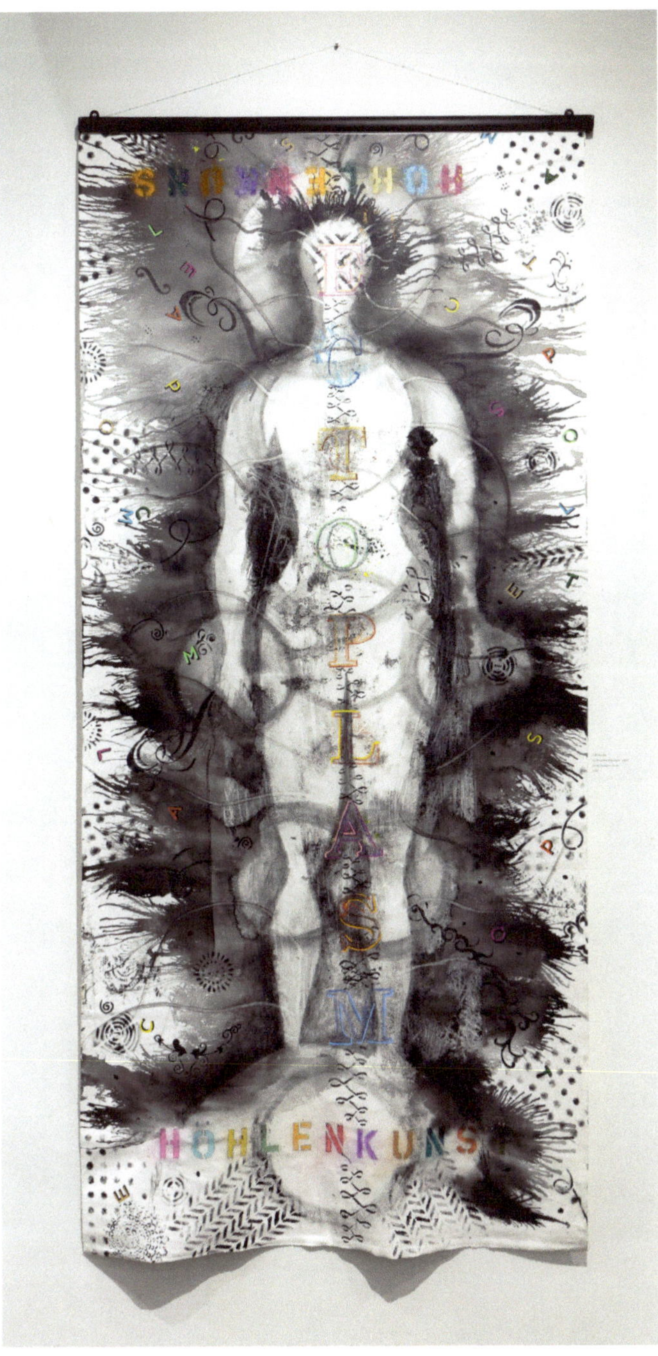

Hohlenkunst

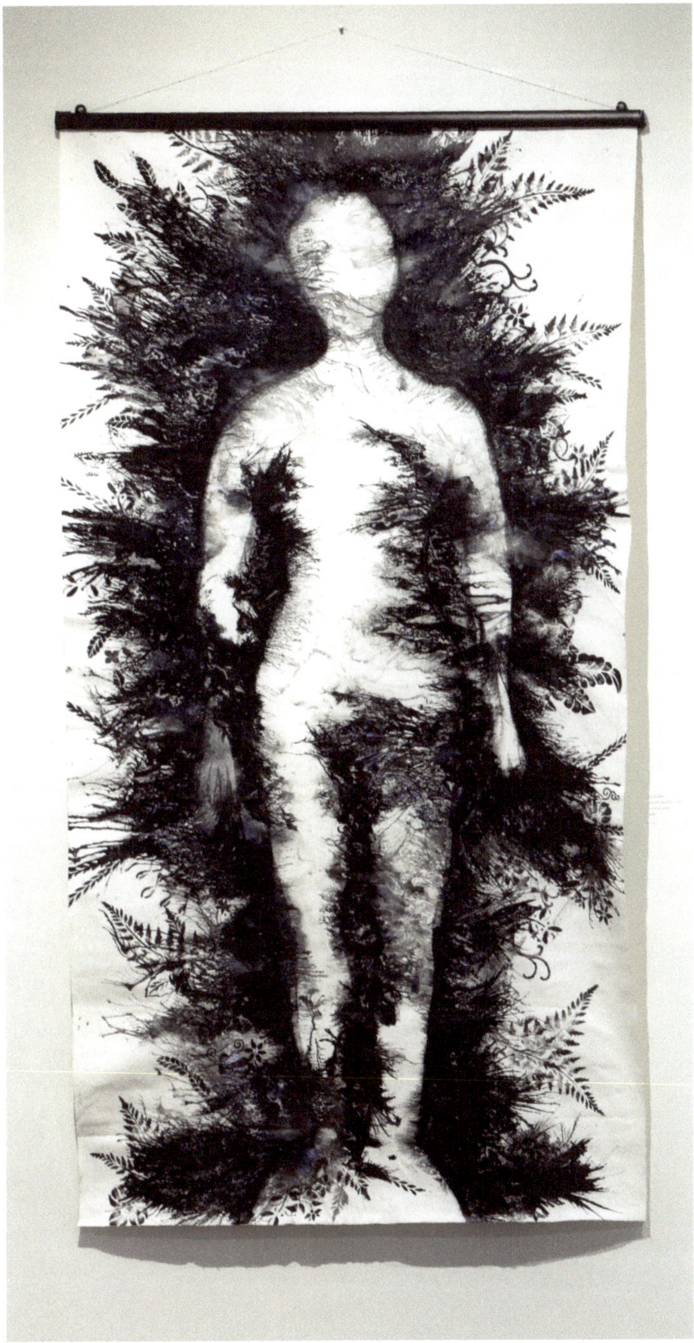

White Fern Ghost

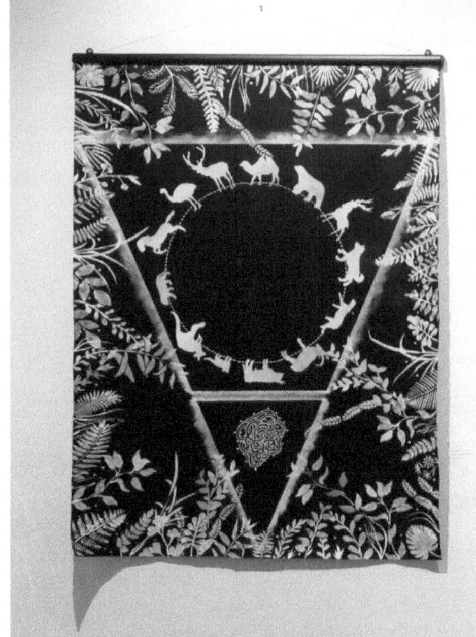

Alchemy Water

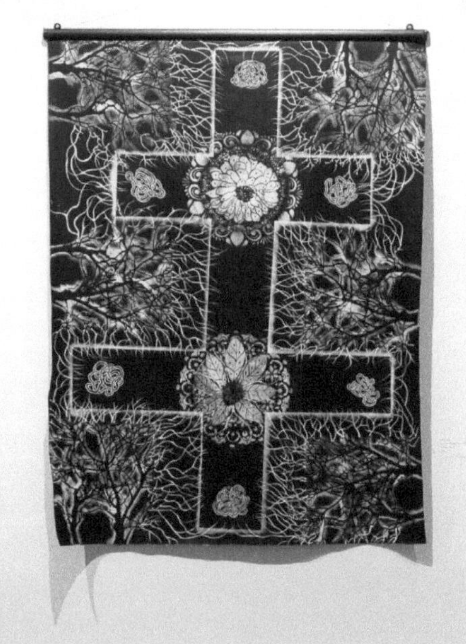

Eastern

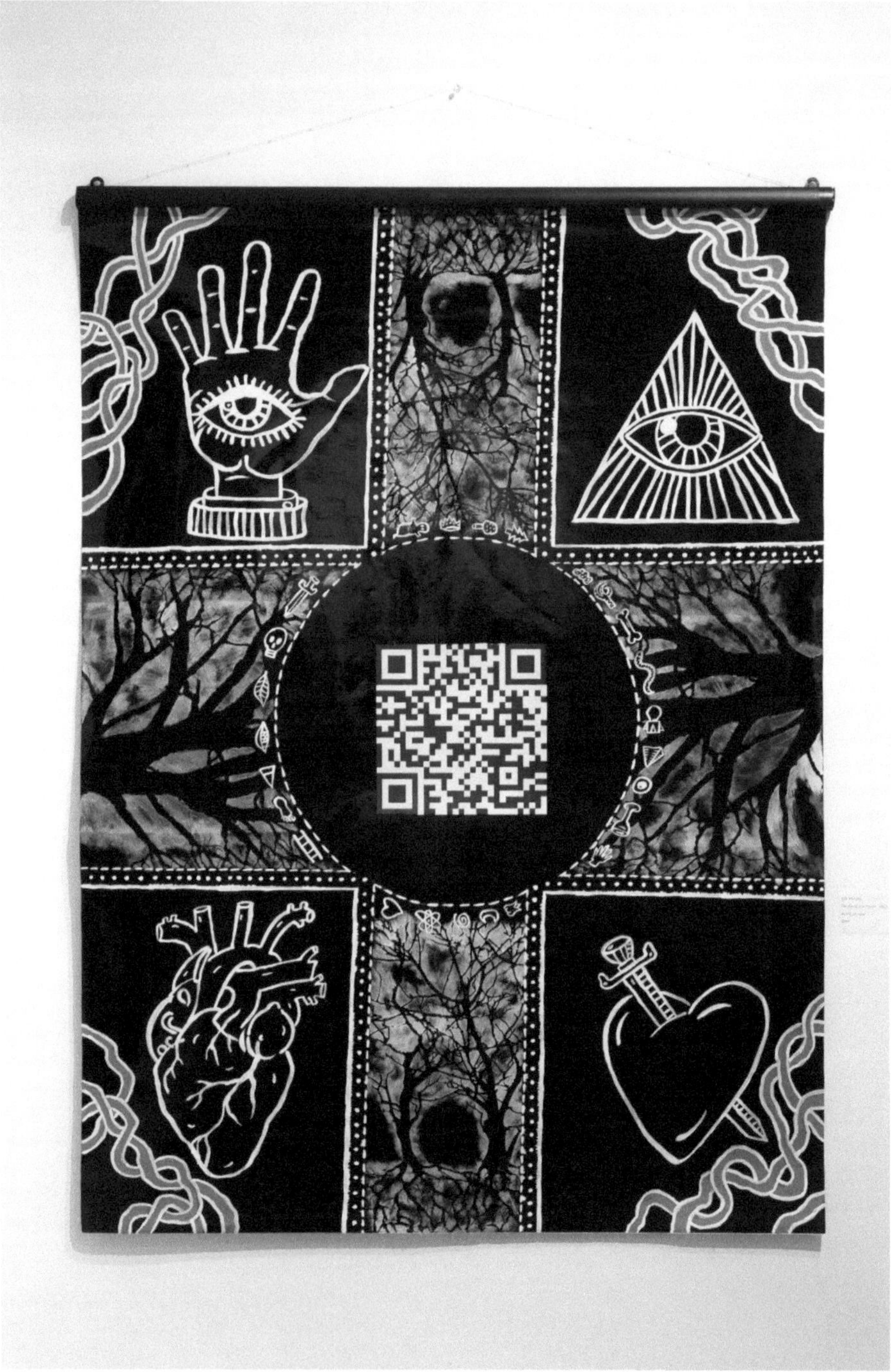

Futurama

MAGICAL CHARTS

Another area of interest to C. B. Murphy are the attempts people have made over centuries and throughout many cultures to depict or graph the meaning of life and the afterlife. Drawing on occult, anthropological history, and pure fantasy, Murphy takes us into a world of somewhat recognizable images (e.g. stencils of animals and plants) which cavort together in an ultimately untranslatable cartography of a world we will never be able to grasp. Like looking at documents from an ancient civilization, we see these Magical Charts for their beauty and accept there is (or might be) a logic underneath that would help us understand life itself, if only we had the key code.

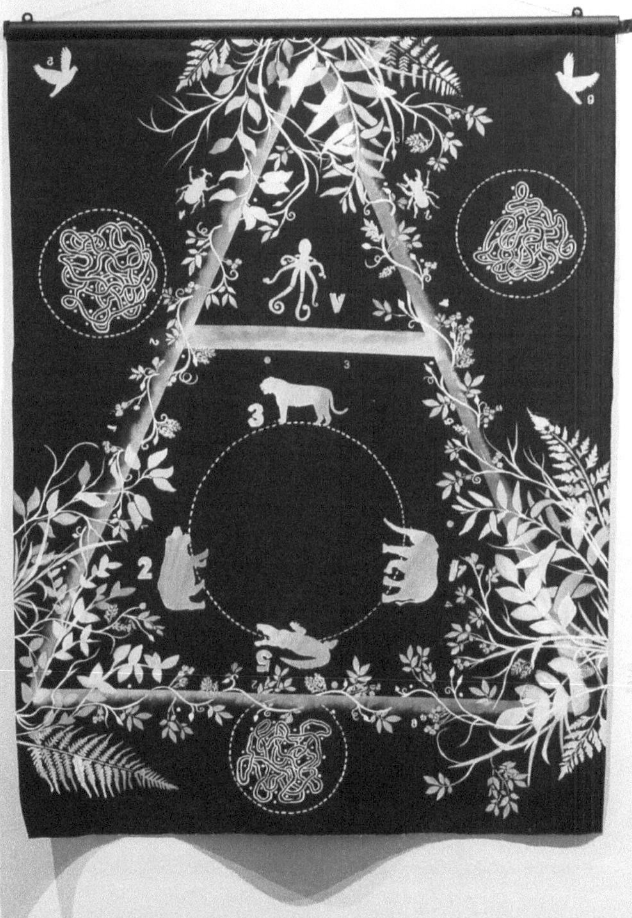

Alchemy Air

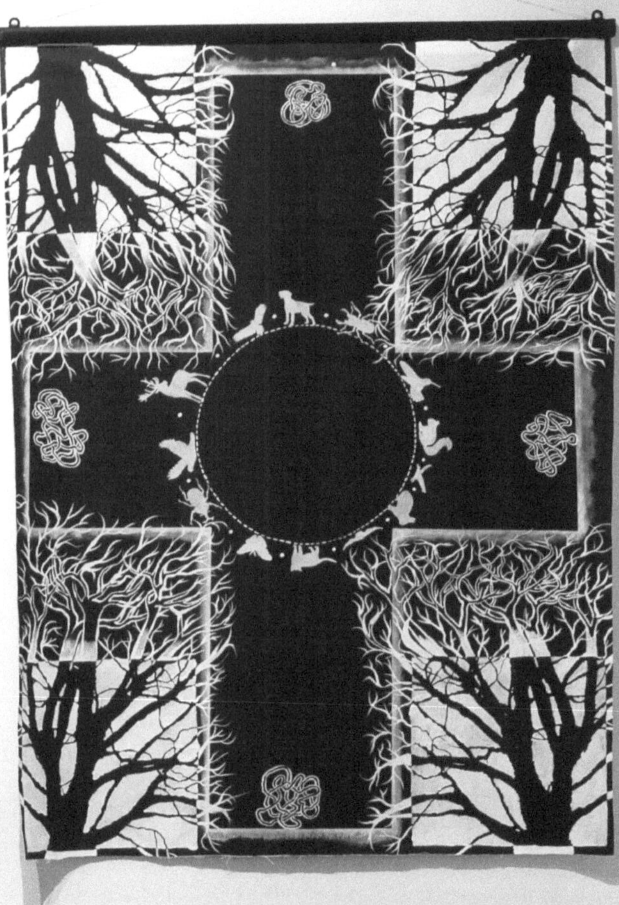

Cross

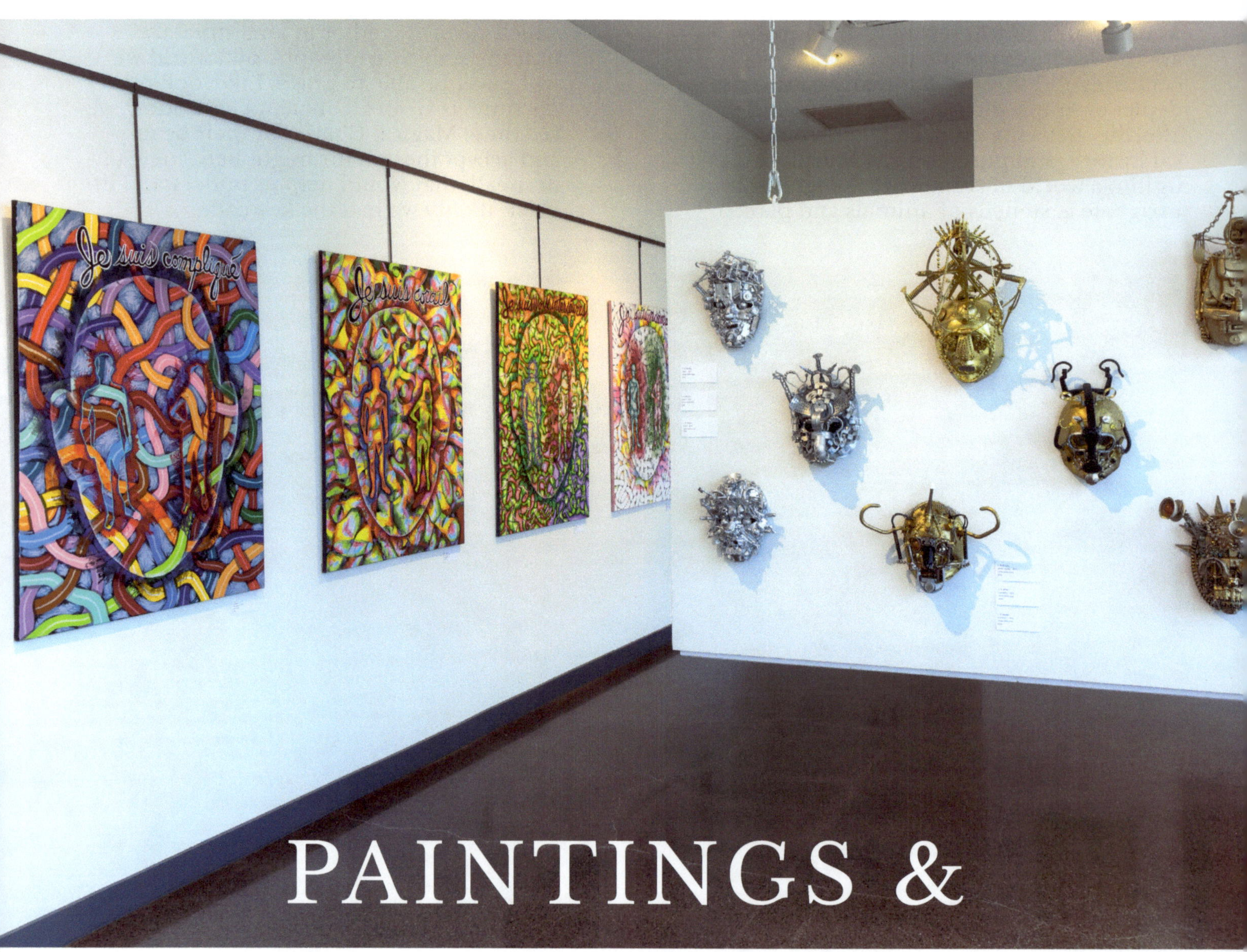

PAINTINGS &

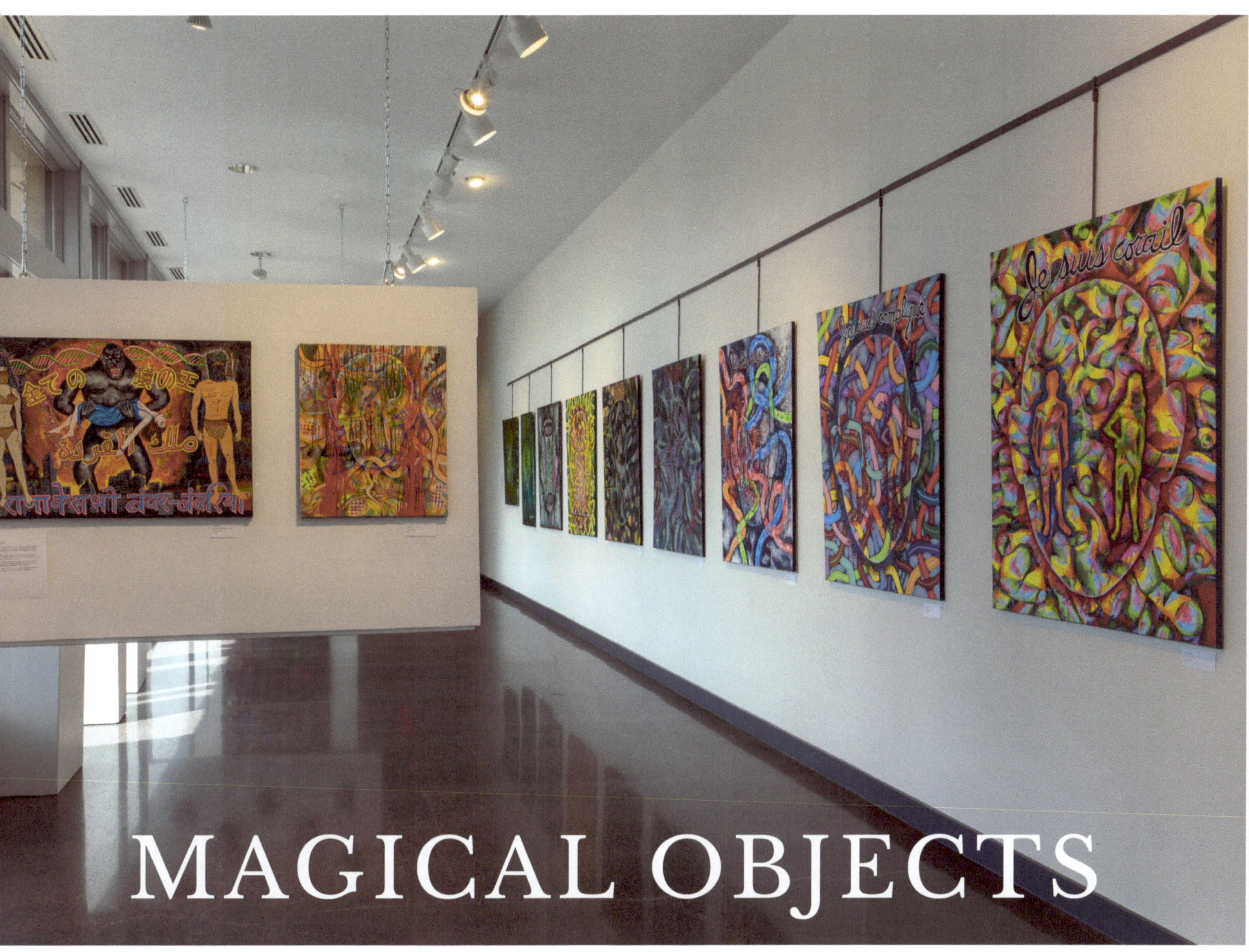

MAGICAL OBJECTS

Phipps Center for the Arts, Hudson, WI 5/6/19—6/16/19

Je Suis: Tamil
Acrylic on Canvas
24" x 36"

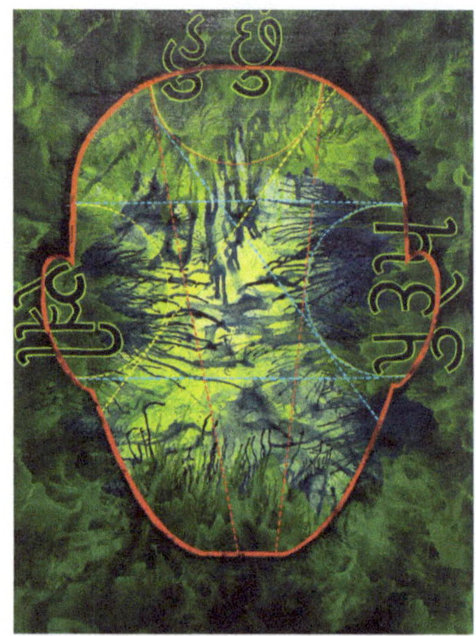

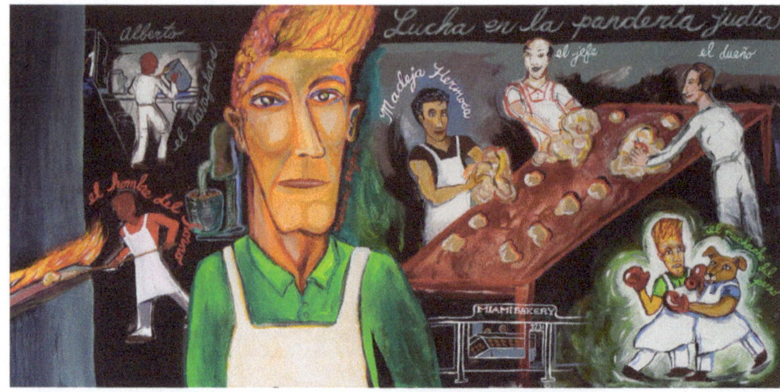

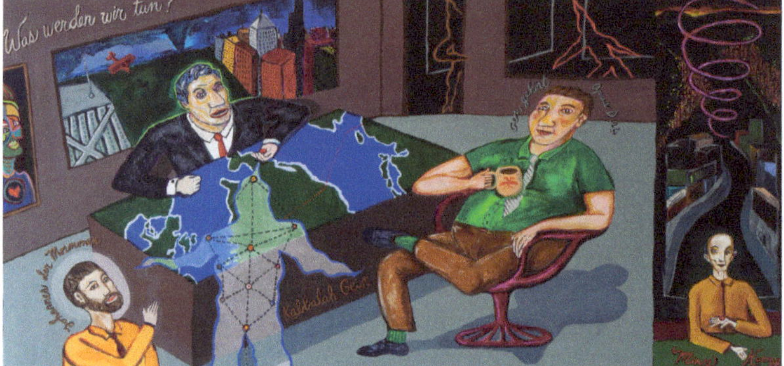

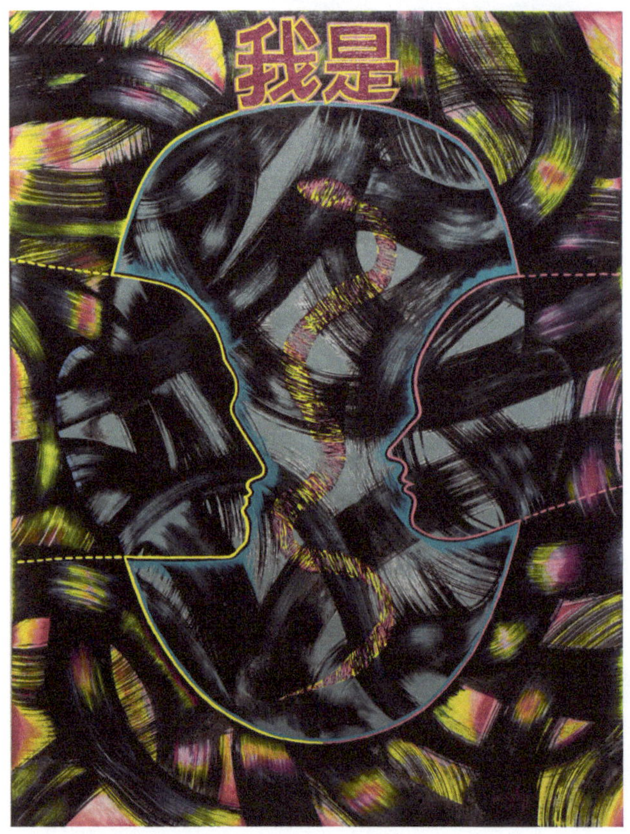

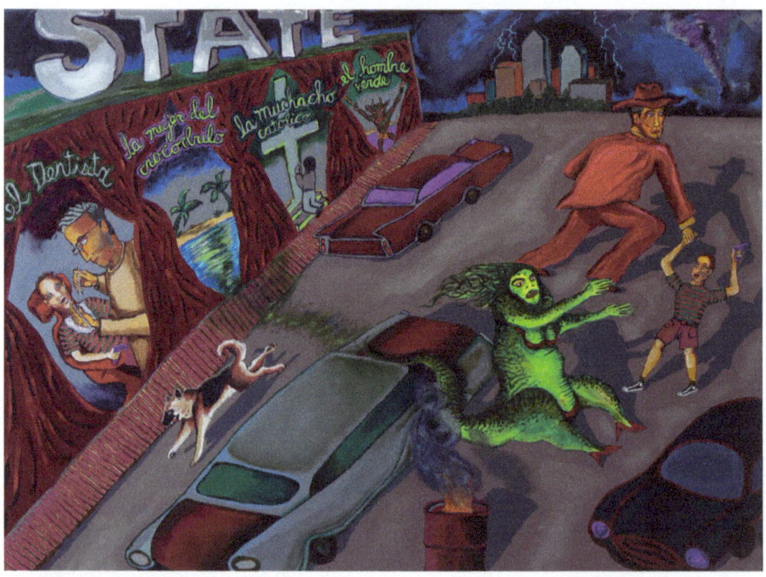

Je Suis: Mandarin
Acrylic on Canvas I 24" x 36"

Memoir Series: Bakery, Hong Kong, State Fair
Acrylic on Canvas I 24" x 36" (3)

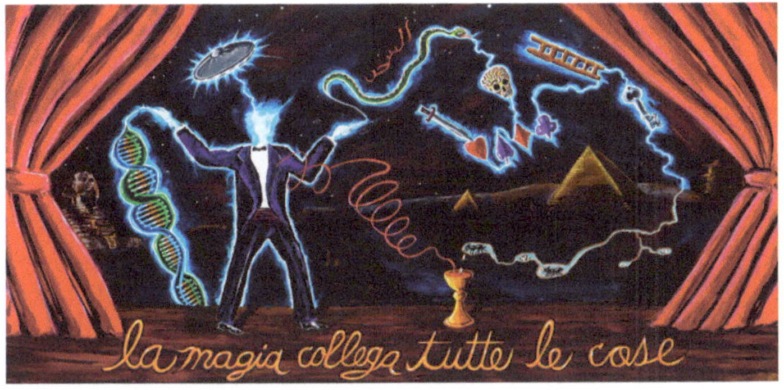

Magic Series: La Magia
Acrylic on Canvas I 24" x 36"

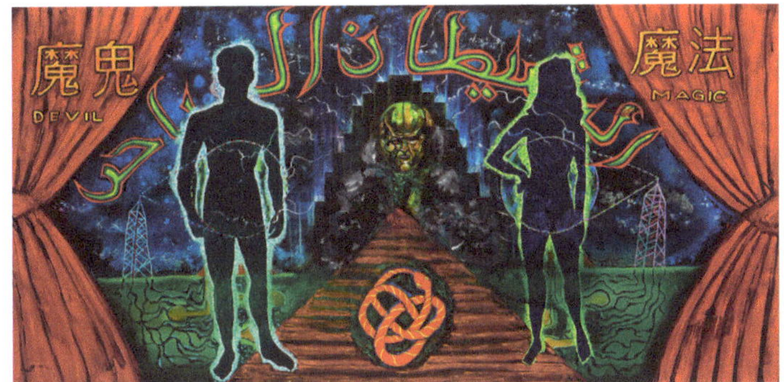

Magic Series: Oz
Acrylic on Canvas I 24" x 36"

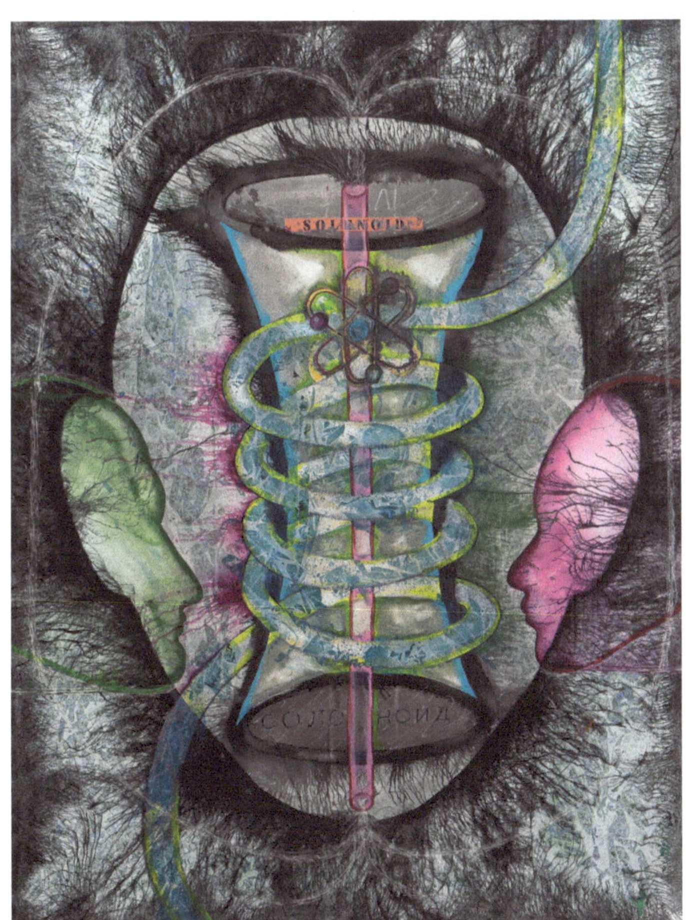

Je Suis: Machine
Acrylic on Canvas I 48" x 36"

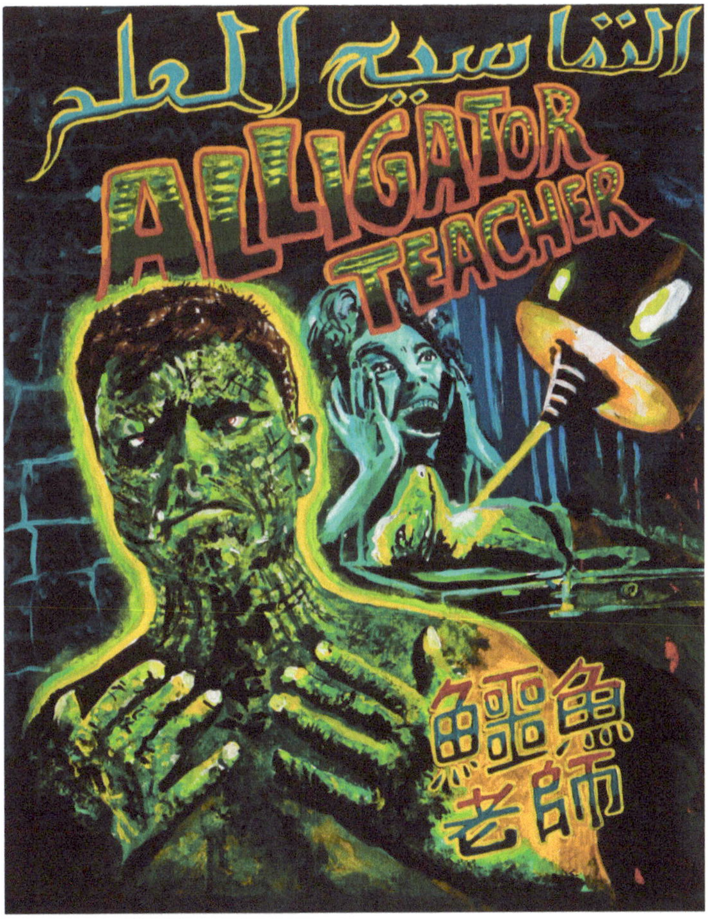

Science Fiction Series: Alligator Teacher
Acrylic on Canvas I 20" x 16"

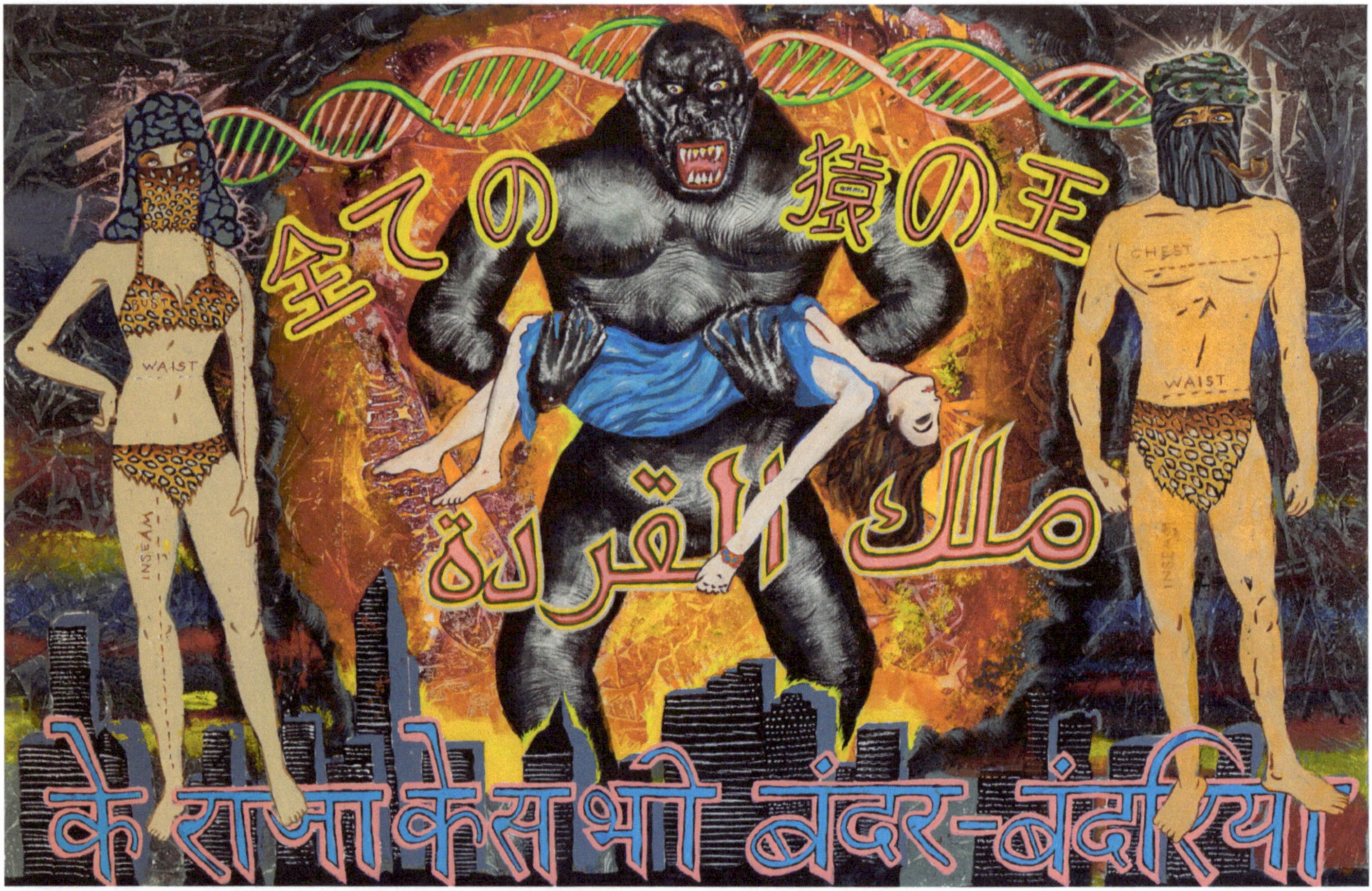

King Kong
Acrylic on Canvas | 24" x 36"

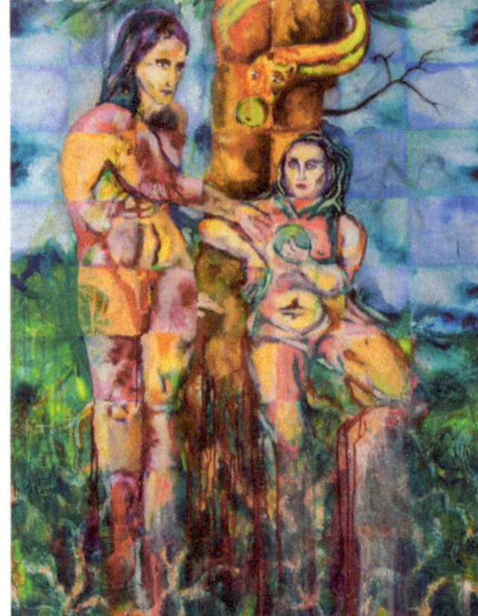

Melting
Acrylic on Canvas | 48"x 36"

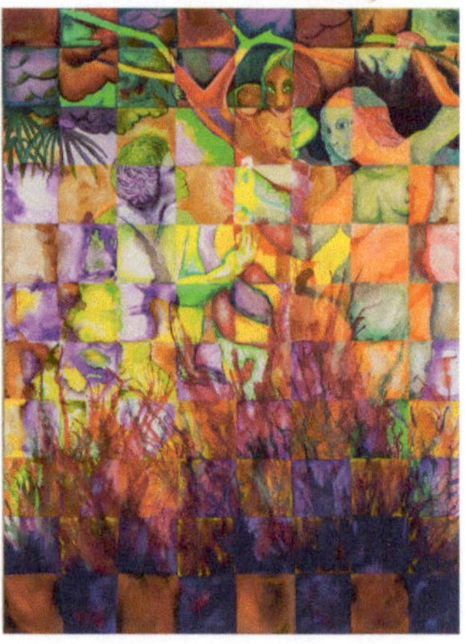

Fire
Acrylic on Canvas | 48" x 36"

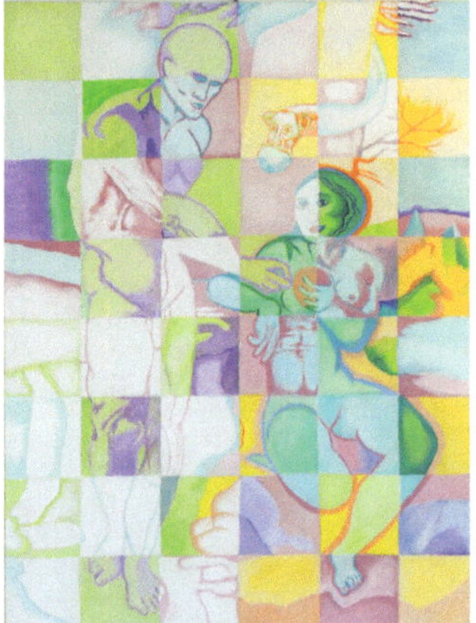

Cubes
Acrylic on Canvas | 48" x 36"

ADAM AND EVE SERIES

I am interested in the many renditions of the story of Adam and Eve over the centuries. It fascinates me that so much has changed and yet many things have not.

Grounding this series on these famous etchings and paintings, I am exploring homage, improvisation, and how my mind in 2019 connects to the past.

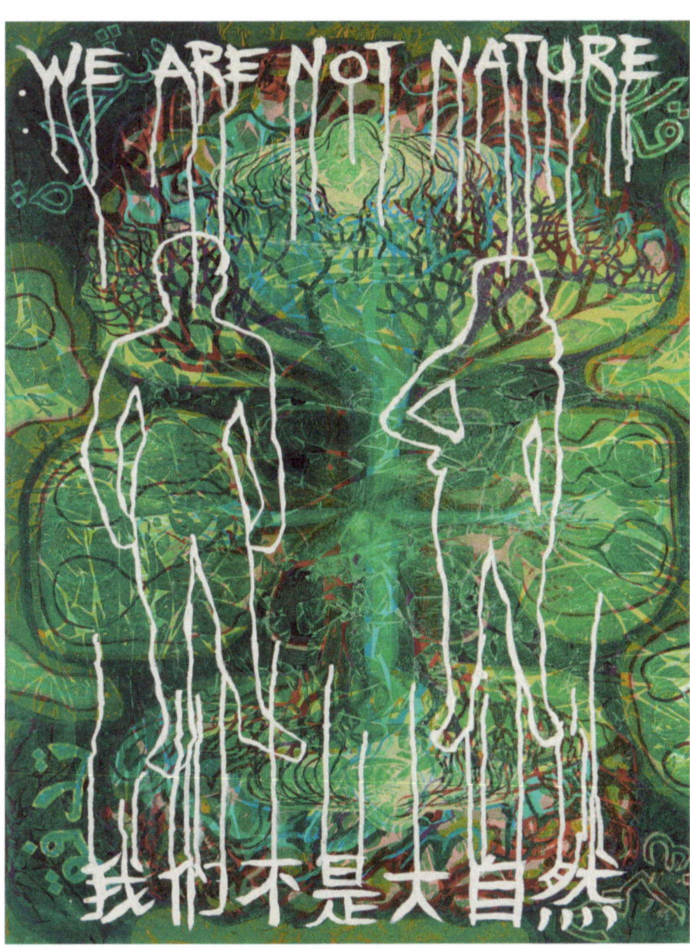

We Are Not Nature I
Acrylic on Canvas I 30" x 24"

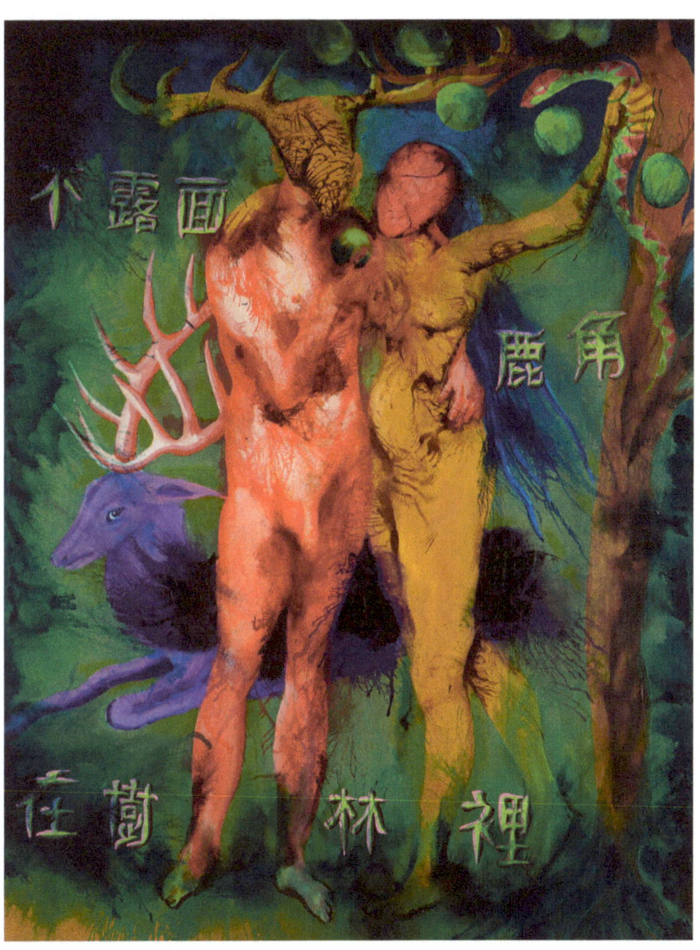

Antlers
Acrylic on Canvas I 48" x 36"

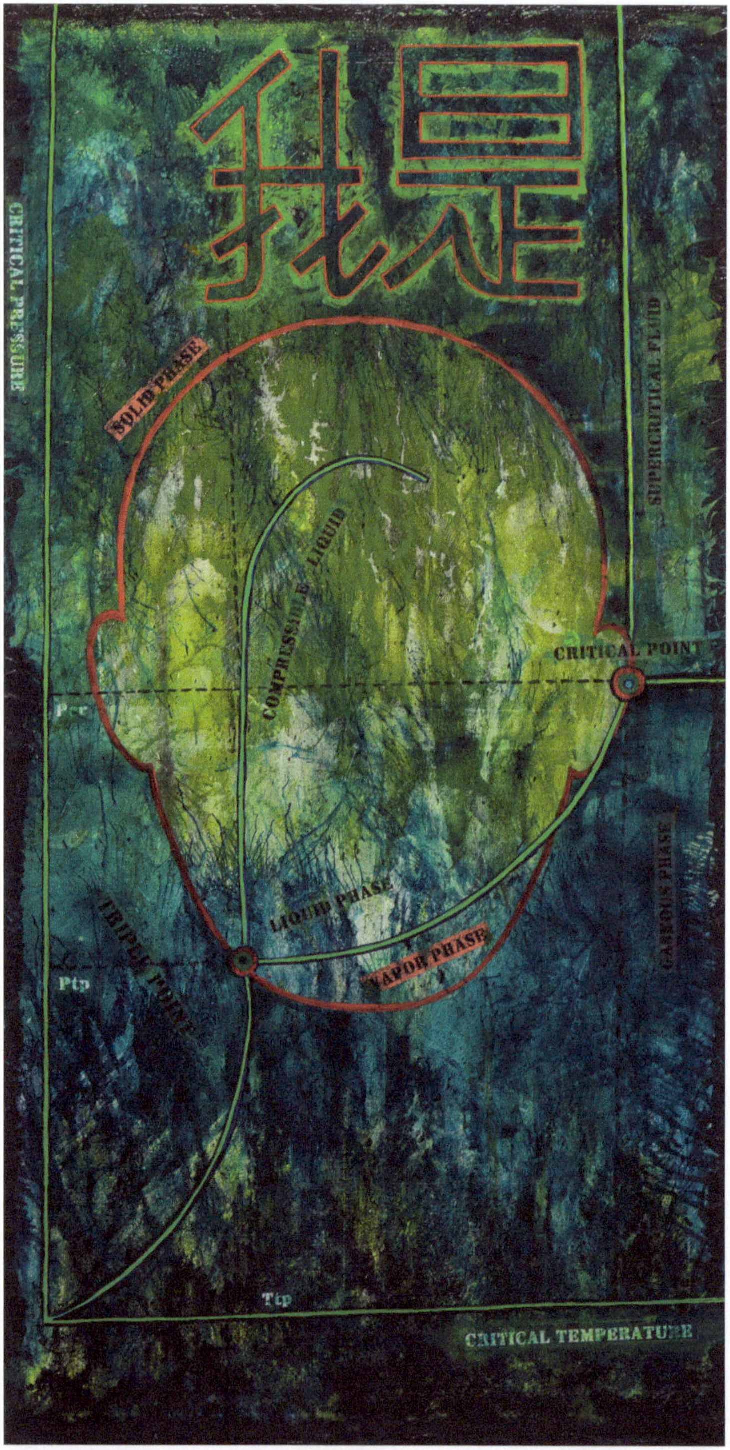

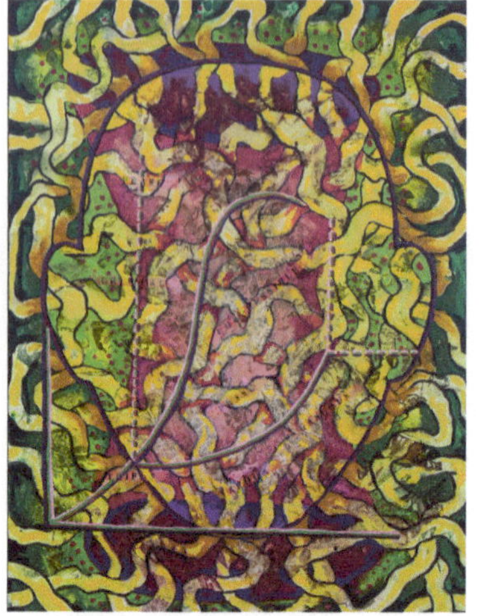

Phase Transition
Acrylic on Canvas
48" x 36"

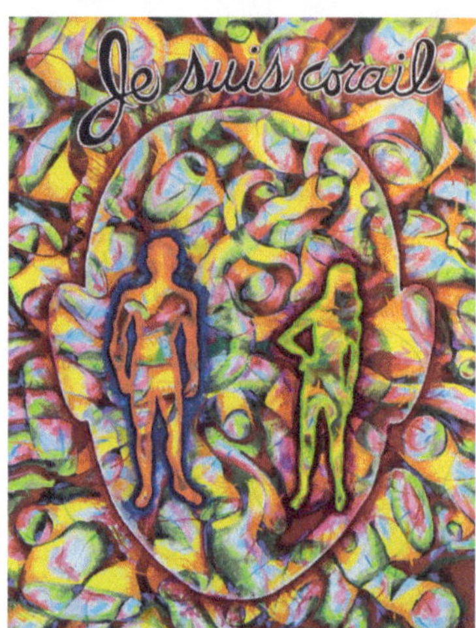

Phase Transition II
Acrylic on Canvas
48" x 36"

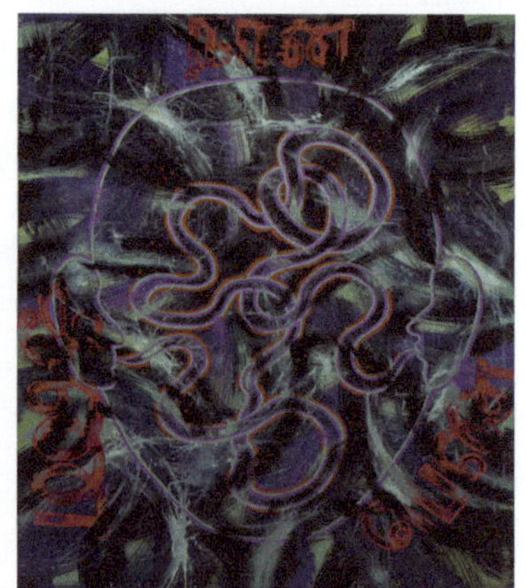

Corail
Acrylic on Canvas
48" x 36"

Gujarati
(Left) Acrylic on Canvas
48" x 36"

JE SUIS SERIES

The "Je Suis" grew out of the Adam and Eve series. Each painting starts with a layer of activity such as intertwining lines, a representation of atomic or genetic activity we cannot perceive in daily life. The second layer is the most basic human element, the outline of a human face. Inside this head are two classically rendered images of male and female, the archetypes that C. G. Jung calls the anima and animus. The fourth level is the "Je Suis/I am" phrase embracing the incomprehensible and the universal. This phrase is rendered in various graphically rich languages binding us together in the complex web we experience as consciousness. Thoughts and feelings, inner archetypes, and the mystery of language bound together in a world sometimes ordered sometimes chaotic.

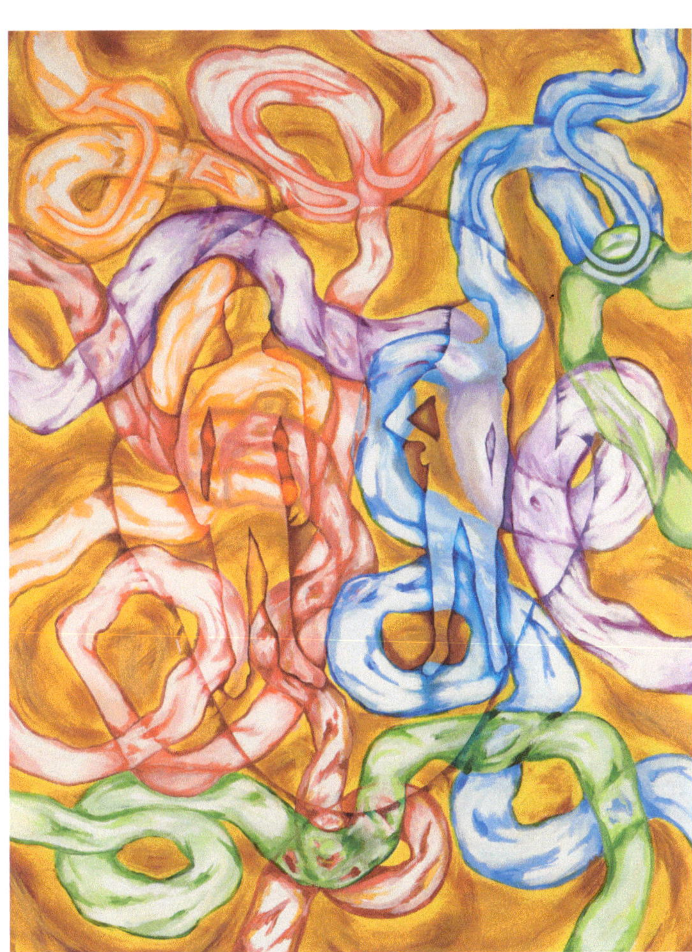

Whirls
Acrylic on Canvas I 48" x 36"

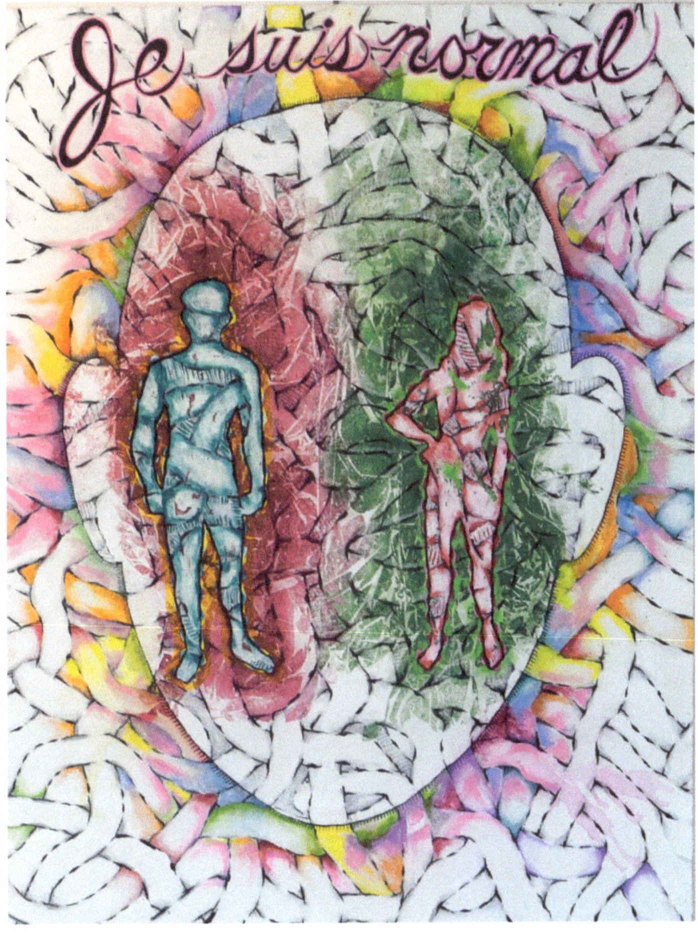

Normal
Acrylic on Canvas I 48" x 36"

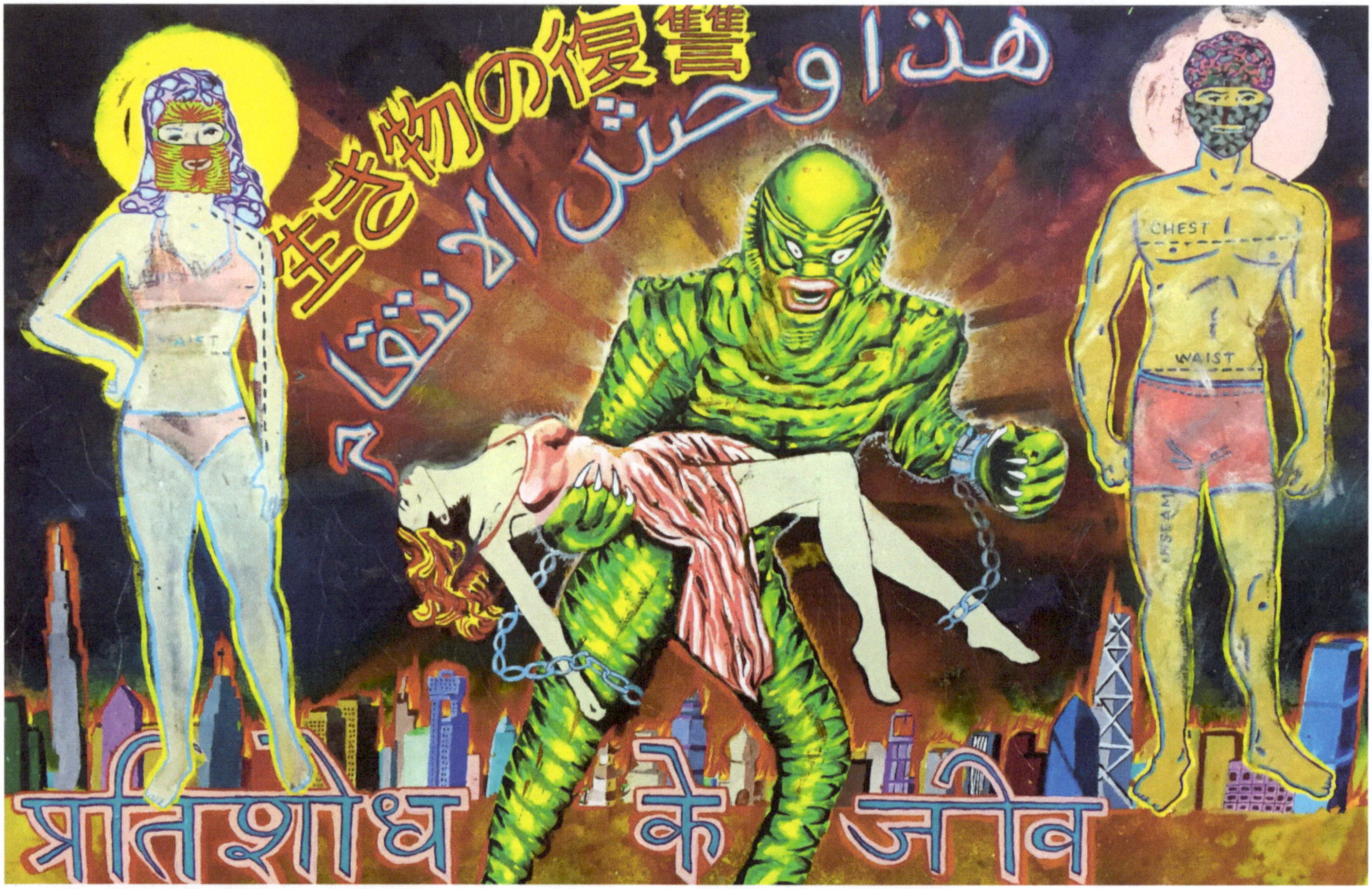

Lagoon
Acrylic on Canvas I 24" x 36"

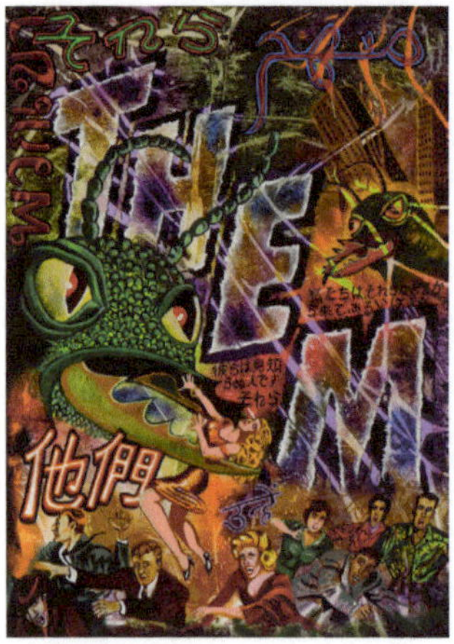

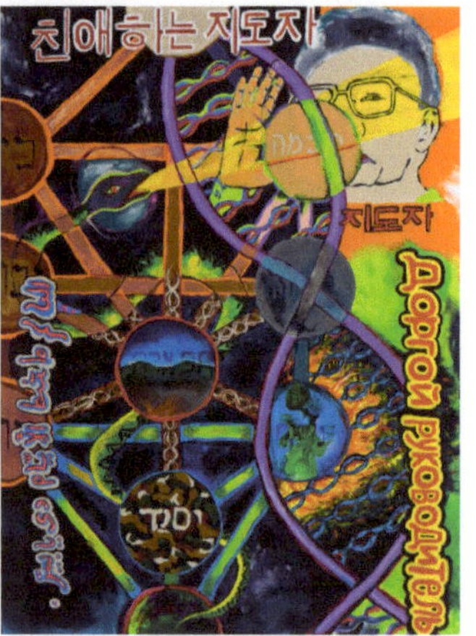

Them
Acrylic on Canvas I 48" x 36"

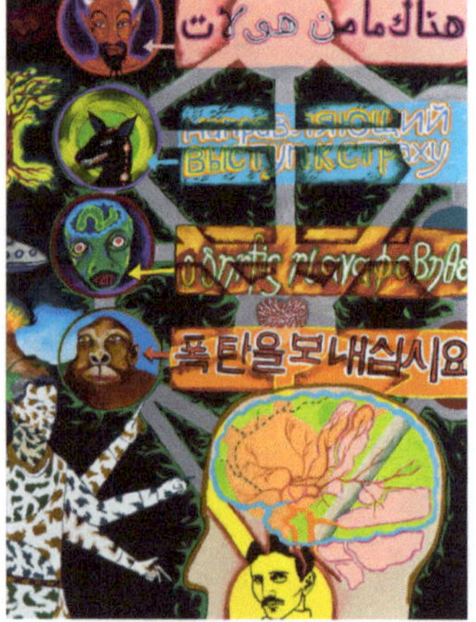

Kim Kabbalah
Acrylic on Canvas I 48" x 36"

Mesmer Kabbalah
Acrylic on Canvas I 48" x 36"

SCIENCE FICTION SERIES

These paintings are an homage to both the movies I loved as a child and continue to enjoy today. The awe, mystery and horror of B-Movies reflects the complex and sometimes frightening situation of humanity, as much today as when they were made.

The Creature From The Black Lagoon is both monster and metaphor conjured from our minds. We sit in the dark, grateful that we are not the young woman the Creature carries into the cave though we know we are.

My idea in using these images as a starting point is that they are "world posters" (Chinese, Arabic, Korean) that have traveled far and been well used. They are the "weathered" posters on the side of a small theater in rural Ghana.

Some of the paintings displayed here connect to both the ADAM AND EVE SERIES and the JE SUIS SERIES by use of the same iconic male and female figures witnessing the events.

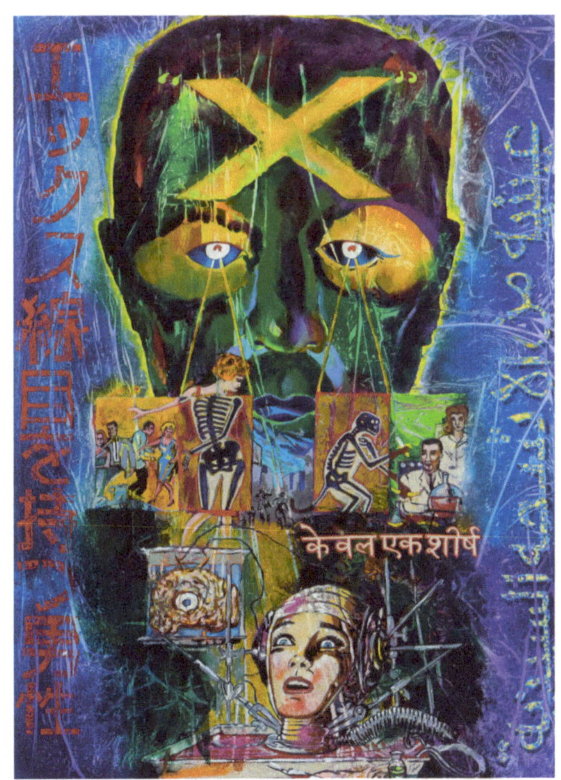

Mr. X
Acrylic on Canvas | 48" x 24"

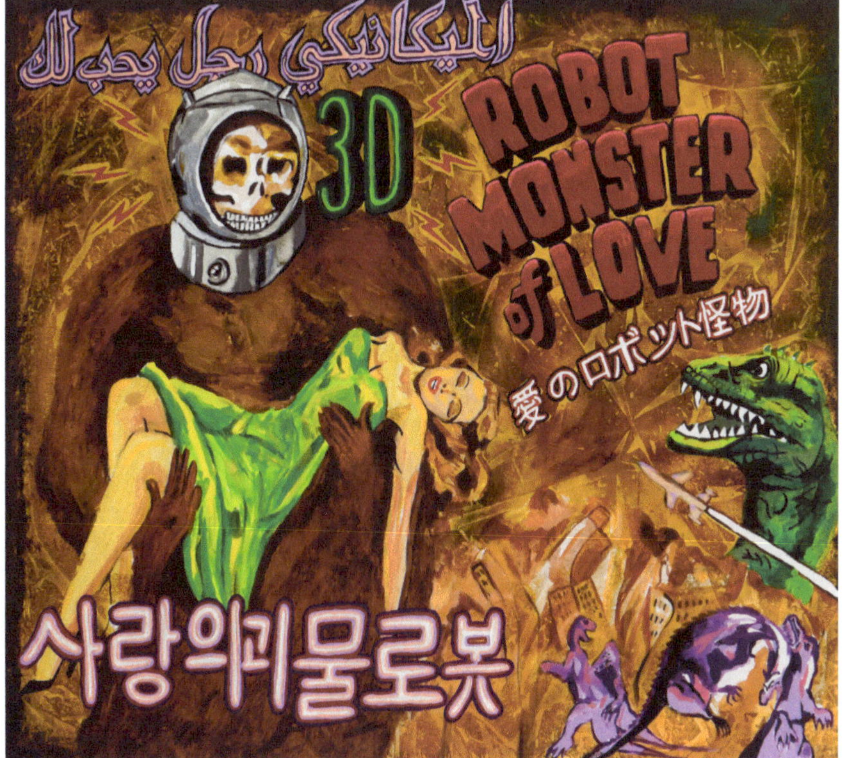

Robot Monster of Love
Acrylic on Canvas | 24" x 24"

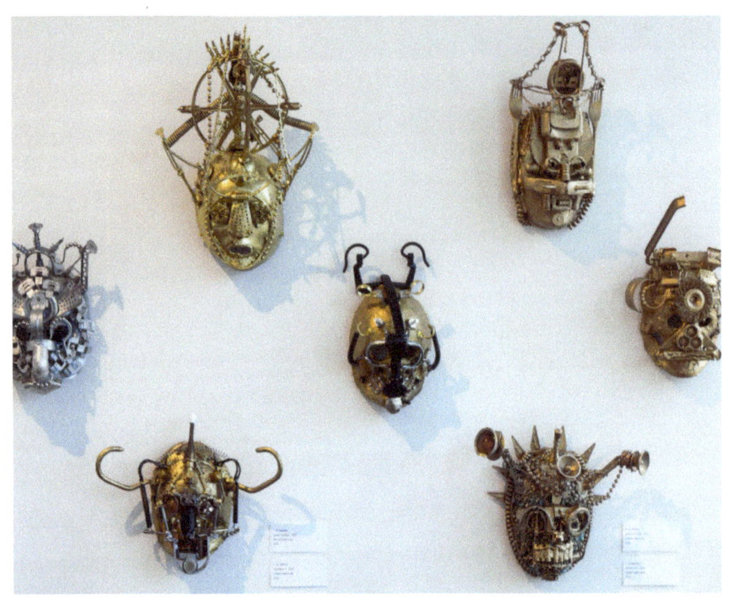
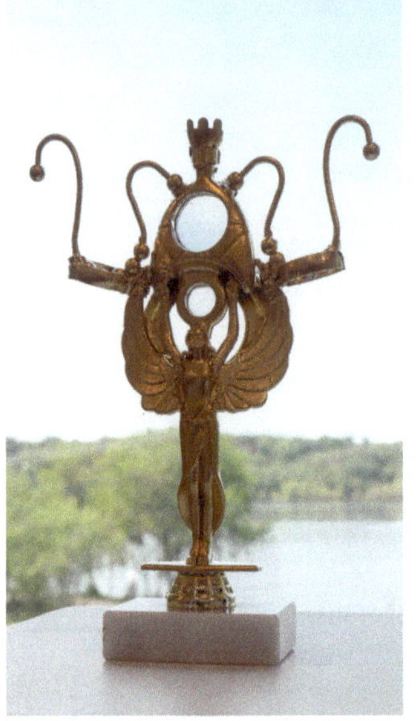
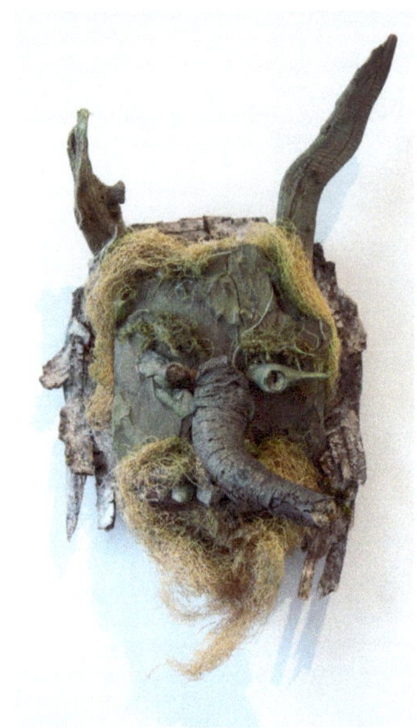
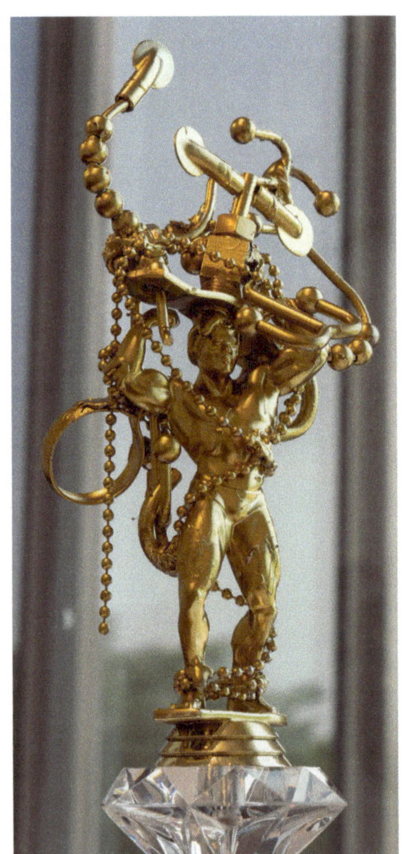
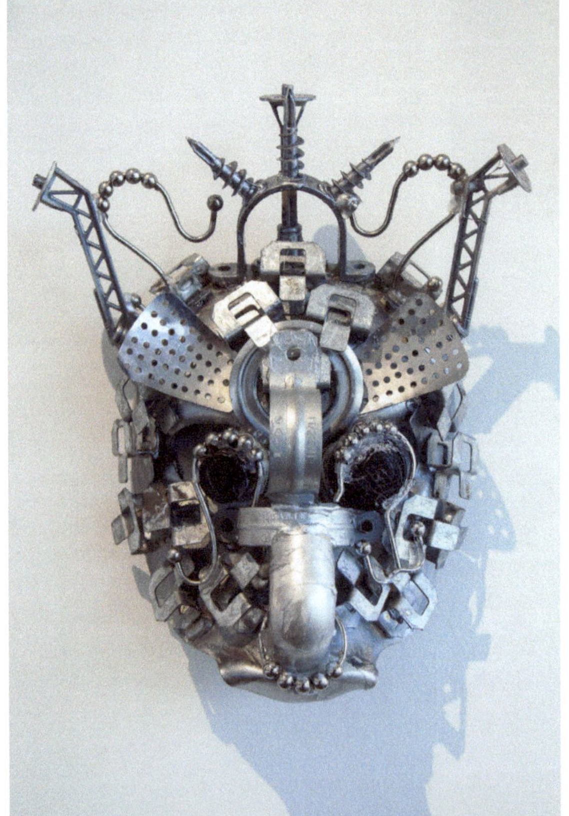
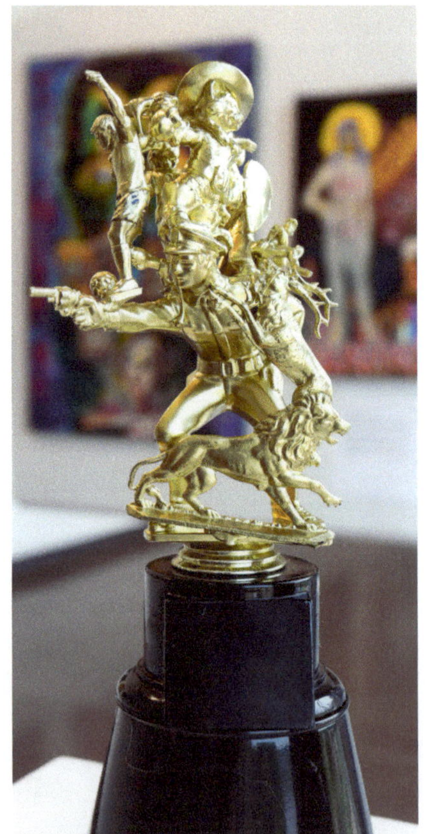

MAGICAL OBJECTS

Murphy creates small sculptures of masks and trophies with found objects. Some use natural materials like wood, bones, and shells, while others draw on a bricolage of industrial detritus. The masks range from the cultish to the science fictional, while the trophies suggest awards might be given for a much wider range of skills than is normally envisioned. Why not an incomprehensible trophy for merely being alive?

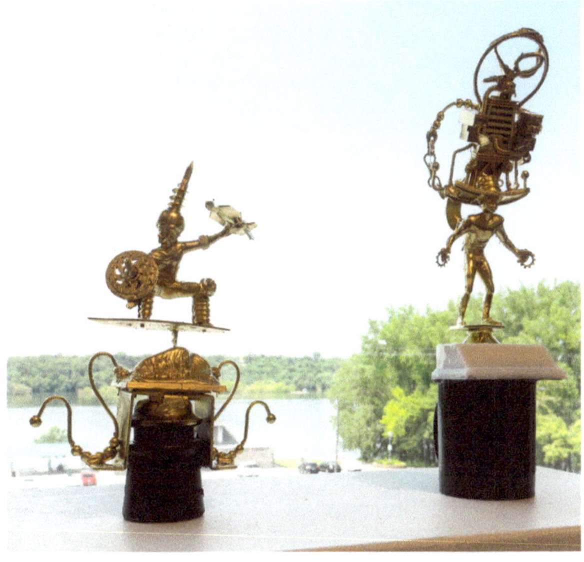

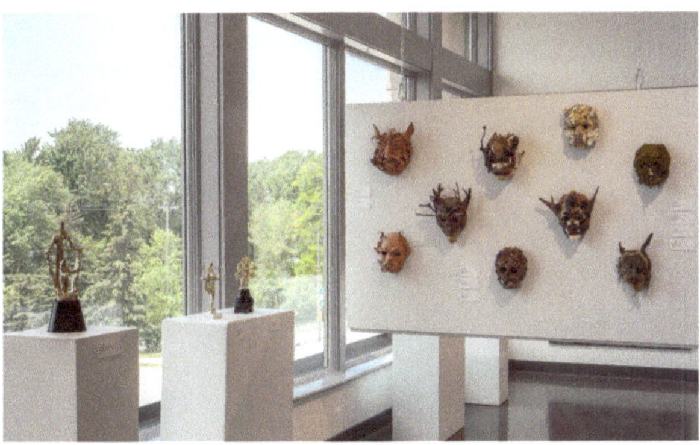

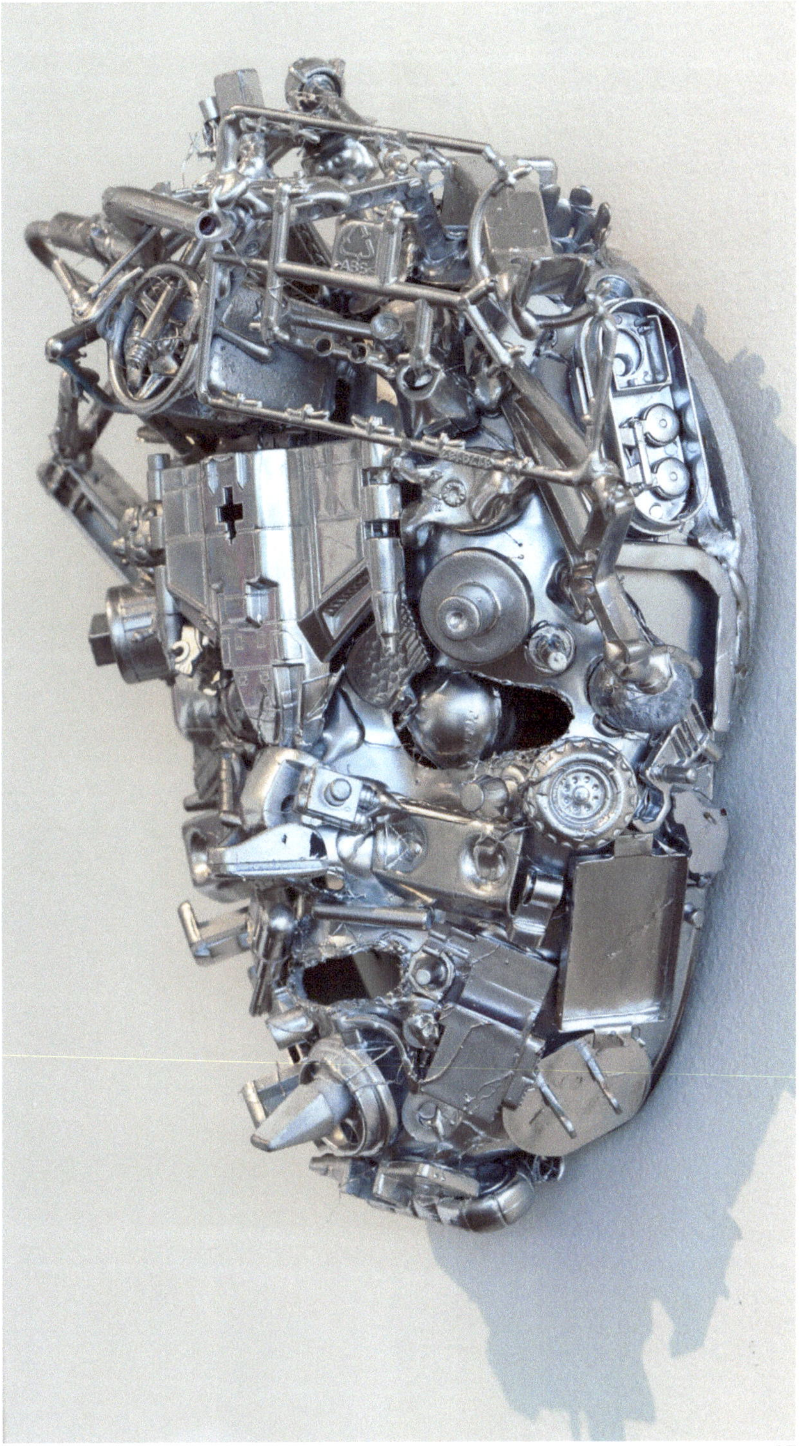

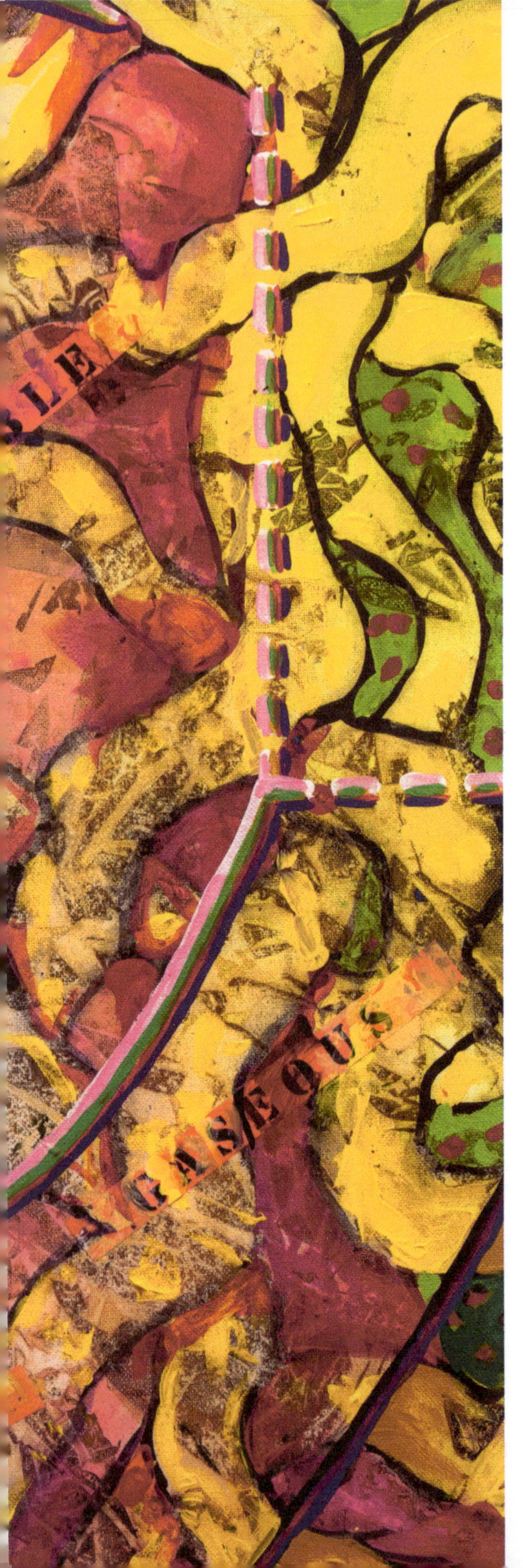

ARTIST STATEMENT

Murphy's art is a conversation between interior realities (feelings, thoughts, dreams) and the collective unconscious (pop culture, classic archetypes, science, history). Painting is a way he connects with human history but also a private meditation on consciousness.

Murphy's paintings are characterized by complex layering of graphic components and meanings. He borrows freely from the charts and graphs with which we explain the world, including science diagrams such as the phase transition of water, and the iconography of alchemists and metaphysicians who attempt to graph what it means to be human.

THE PHIPPS
CENTER FOR THE ARTS

The Phipps has celebrated the creative spirit since 1983 by offering exciting theater, dance, and concert performances, engaging gallery exhibitions, and inspiring instruction in the performing and visual arts. Discover the distinctive energy that makes the Phipps a regional treasure in the St. Croix Valley. The spirited blend of performances, exhibitions, and classes ensures an accessible artistic experience for everyone. The Phipps welcomes you to explore the arts.

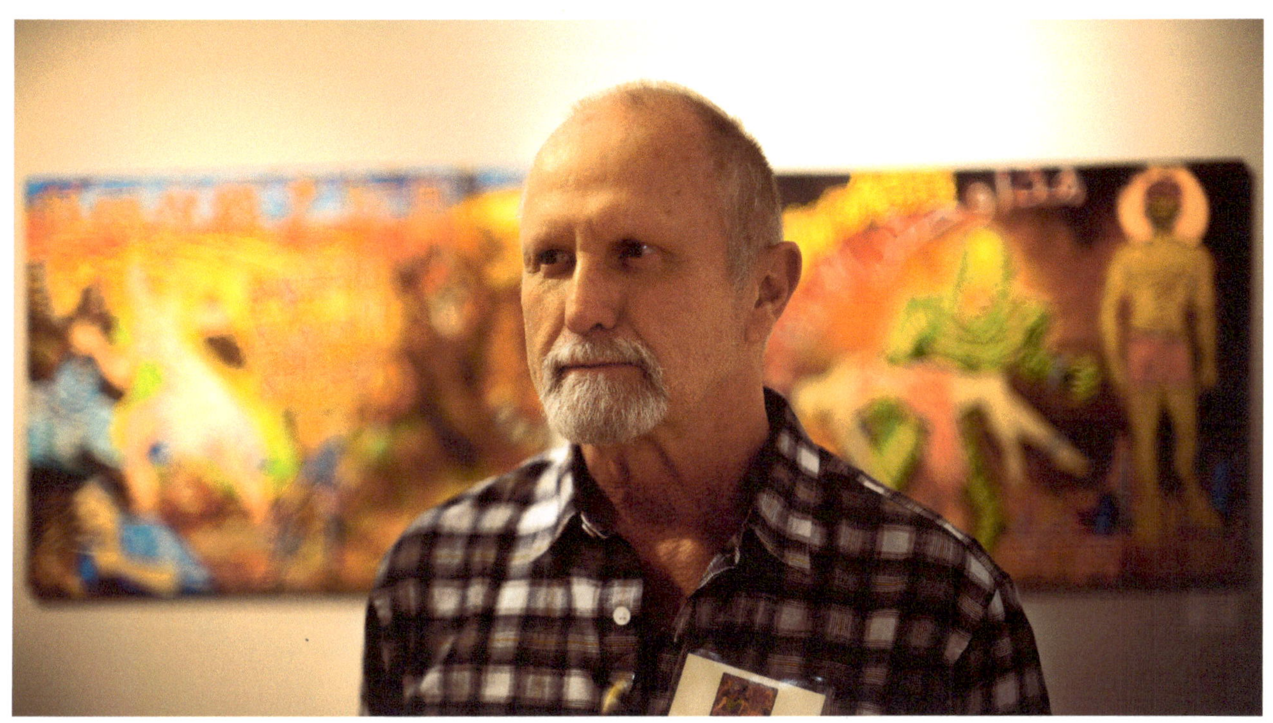

612.723.8790

charleybmurphy@gmail.com

www.cbmurphy.net

Instagram @cb_murphy

Price and availability on request

ABOUT C.B. MURPHY

Charley (CB) Murphy of Marine on St. Croix, MN, is a painter, mixed media artist, sculptor, and novelist. Murphy has worked in marketing, product development, illustration, film-making, cartooning, and art education. For ten years he has been a volunteer art teacher at Stillwater Correctional Facility, Bayport, MN. His work has been shown all across the United States.

www.ingramcontent.com/pod-product-compliance
Lightning Source LLC
Chambersburg PA
CBHW042137030726
47599CB00002B/515